What is Good Government in Asia?

What is Good Government in Asia?

Publisher Ki-Pung Yoo
Director Chanje Wu

Edited by Youngho Cho

Published in Sogang University Press
35 Baekbeom-ro, Mapo-gu, Seoul 04107, Korea
Tel +82-2-705-8212 Fax +82-2-705-8612

ISBN 978-89-7273-312-6 93300
₩13,000

What is Good Government in Asia?

Edited by

Youngho Cho

SOGANG UNIVERSITY PRESS

This research was supported by Social Science Korea program through the National Research Foundation of Korea(NRF) funded by the Ministry of Education(NRF-2013S1A3A2055205).

Preface

This book arose as part of an ongoing project, "Good Government in South Korea," initiated in 2011 by Hyeon-Woo Lee, director of the Sogang Institute of Political Studies (SIPS). Good government is not a new topic among political theories and comparative politics, but it is something that ordinary people have dreamed of and politicians have sought. Accordingly, scholars have examined the nature, causes, and consequences of good government across countries and in history. Recently, three scholars—Robert Putnam, Bo Rothstein, and Francis Fukuyama—explicitly raised the centrality of good government in guaranteeing civil peace, sustaining social prosperity, and preventing socioeconomic and political decay. Their efforts notwithstanding, there is a lack of theoretical and empirical studies on good government in Asia. This project is an effort to expand our understanding of good government in general and the quality of Asian governments specifically.

Over the years, the good government program of the SIPS has investigated procedures and institutions with which to improve the quality of government in South Korea. In particular, the SIPS team has found that the South Korean government has a strong bureaucratic traditions in the world, but it is not effective in responding to citizens' diverse demands. The team has identified factors that prevent the government from becoming a high-quality and responsive one. These include overgrown bureaucratic power, weak democratic accountability, and strong presidentialism. Having experienced state-directed development in the shadow of the North Korean communist threat, South Korea is a country where a president with a single term employs both bureaucracy and a ruling party to set and drive the national agendas. Because the development of democratic institutions has been sluggish in constraining government-driven initiatives and in making them accountable and responsive to public demands, there is a significant gap between what citizens want and what government supplies. Strong presidentialism creates an opportunity structure in which organized interest groups make inroads into government decision making and bureaucratic elites wield autonomous authority over specific policies. Building on these findings, the SIPS team raises questions about good government in other Asian countries having similar colonialist histories, cultures, and developmental trajectories in common. Do Asian countries have similar problems with the quality of government? What are specific issues of good government for individual Asian countries?

To examine these questions in a comparative perspective, the SIPS gathered some of the prominent scholars of comparative politics and Asian studies at an international conference called "What Is Good Government in Asia?" sponsored by the National Research Foundation of South Korea, which met in Seoul on April 29, 2016. This brought together a distinguished group of scholars to compare states of good government in six Asian countries: Japan, China, Indonesia, Vietnam, Malaysia, and South Korea. We had valuable discussions and appreciate the National Research Foundation for facilitating this conference. In addition, we are thankful to everyone who participated as presenters, moderators, and discussants, including Benny Teh Cheng Guan, Willy Jou, Abdul Malik Gismar, Lingling Qi, Tran Van Kham, Yoon-hwan Shin, Myoungsei Kang, Eun Hong Park, Han Woo Lee, Jaehyon Lee, Jae Hyeok Shin, Euisuok Han, Wooyeal Paik, Jiwon Suh, and Djayadi Hanan.

Youngho Cho
Sogang University, South Korea
May 18, 2016

Contents

Part 2. Good Government in Northeast Asia

1

Introduction: Centrality of Good Government in Asia

Youngho Cho
Sogang University, South Korea

The two world wars in the twentieth century left two irreversible legacies for the development of modern government. The two great wars and warfare during the interwar period gave modern government in advanced countries the ability to extract social and economic resources from society to the maximum degree and focus them on specific government goals under the bureaucratic and rational calculation. Due to the wars and warfare, modern government in major countries possessed the most autonomous and capable power, which Huntington (1968) called *political development and institutionalization*. On the other hand, the most destructive world wars dramatically weakened major Western and non-Western states so that the major countries could not help but liberate their colonies. Right after the end of WWII, former colonial countries in Asia, Africa, and the Middle East declared independence and adopted the Western model of modern government. During the 1950s–1960s, the number of independent countries skyrocketed from one hundred to about two hundred. Accordingly, modern government, invented and advanced in the West, has become a global phenomenon.

Since then, political discourse on good government has been followed a circuitous path and wandered. In the 1950s and 1960s, modern governments in the developed world commonly announced grand social programs and introduced various welfare policies including national pension, national health insurance, unemployment insurance, and occupational health and safety insurance. Even in the United States, where weak government is a tradition and liberalism was a social and political principle, Kennedy and Johnson promoted Great Society proposals in which government took an active role in eliminating poverty, strengthening public education, and increasing medical care. Overall, good government during this period was a government taking wide social and economic responsibilities. This active and responsible government was exported to newly independent countries and promoted state-directed development, although most of these countries experienced dictatorial rule.

Political discourse on good government shifted during the 1970s and 1980s, first in the Anglo-Saxon countries. Neoliberal scholars such as Friedrich Hayek, Milton Friedman, and Robert Nozick criticized outgrowth of modern government in various perspectives. According to them, because overgrown government cannot have accurate information about citizens' preferences, what they provide is limited in meeting citizens' demands. Overgrown due to the great wars and expanded welfare policies, modern government was perceived not as a solution to social and economic challenges but as a problem itself. In the name of new public management (NPM), scholars and politicians at that time tried their best to reduce government size as well as social and economic responsibility. At the same time, governments in the advanced countries introduced business-like management. A series of reforms in the developed areas helped advanced countries overcome debt problems, economic recovery, and government inefficiency.

However, this neoliberal discourse on good government promoted destructive policies that jeopardized both governments and societies in the developing areas. Low commodity prices in the 1980s nearly collapsed resource-rich economies and the International Monetary Fund and other international organizations imposed austerity policies in Africa, Asia, and Latin America. As the United States stopped supporting its authoritarian allies and the Soviet Union was dissolved and Russia could not sustain its satellite countries abroad, some of the weak governments became self-serving and predatory. Furthermore, in Somalia, Sudan, and Ethiopia, governments failed and states nearly collapsed. Together with the popularity of neoliberalism, declining political trust left limited room for government to take increased responsibility in both developed and developing countries.

Over the last three decades, waves of global democratization have promised that democratic procedures such as elections and multiparty competition would make government accountable to citizens and responsive to their preferences, thereby promoting civil peace and economic prosperity and reducing corruption.

Nonetheless, there is consensus that the democratic waves have had a limited impact on good governance.

Since the 1990s, having observed political discontent and continuous protests in advanced countries and government failure in the developing areas, few scholars have recently advocated small government as good government. Contemporary prominent scholars have reasserted a discourse of responsible government and debated the content of good government in this present era. Robert Putnam (1993) was among the first to investigate good government at both theoretical and empirical levels. In his famous book, *Making Democracy Work*, Putnam explicitly argued that good government is one that actively responds to citizens' various demands. After his groundbreaking case study on Italy, Bo Rothstein and his colleagues in the Quality of Government Institute at Gothenburg University of Sweden have been the most active academic team to drive this topic and conduct extensive research (Charron, Dijkstra, and Lapuente 2015; Holmberg, Rothstein, and Nasiritousi 2009; Rothstein 2011). According to them, good government is impartial. Because modern government receives diverse demands from individuals and social and economic groups, good government must not favor one over another but keep a principle of impartiality in dealing with citizens and making public decisions. Finally, Francis Fukuyama (2011, 2014, 2016) contends that good government has three properties: functioning bureaucracy, democratic accountability, and rule of law. Considering that Fukuyama declared that the end of history and liberal democracy would be the only political alternative for the world's future, his shift toward good government indicates that small government and NPM are nearly over. These scholars together contend that good government in this period is not a small and liberal government, but it should be capable of delivering public goods in response to citizens' demands and be fair in dealing with public affairs.

Within this academic and political discourse, there is a dearth of studies on good government in the non-Western world. Although prior studies have relevant implications for good government and government reforms, there is a lack of studies directly investigating the quality of government in Asia. This book is an effort to expand our understanding about good government in Asia in a comparative perspective. In this book, six scholars examine good government in their countries: Indonesia, Vietnam, Malaysia, China, Japan, and South Korea. Because these six Asian countries have state-directed developmental experiences under authoritarian dictatorship, this book provides a fresh look at the quality of government in the non-Western world. The six experts identify current states of good government in Asia and report interesting findings. Taken together, they investigate barriers behind low-functioning governments and make policy recommendations.

Following this introduction, three authors from Southeast Asia examine the current state of good government in their countries. Dr. Teh reports the quality of the Malaysian government, with a focus on corruption. To examine the key challenges and strategies for anti-corruption, he assumes that corruption not only obstructs good governance or breeds bad government but also that it threatens human lives and social harmony. Specifically, his chapter employs a human security lens by adopting a two-pronged top-down and bottom-up approach to the issue. The top-down approach examines initiatives introduced and anti-corruption strategies employed by the government in line with the notion of good government. Under this approach, the ability of government policies to uphold transparency and accountability in protecting peoples' concerns is discussed. The bottom-up approach looks at a myriad of activities designed to empower individuals and social movements concerned with corruption-related issues to voice their dissatisfactions, generate awareness, and seek redress for better governance. He concludes that both approaches are necessary in combating wide corruption in Malaysian government.

In the next chapter, Dr. Kham develops his original framework to evaluate good governance in Vietnam and compares it with existing indices such as World Governance Indicators. By doing so, he uncovers some hidden dimensions of the Vietnamese government in the perspective of good governance. In particular, since 2010 he has conducted the project Governance and Public Administration Performance Index on six main dimensions of participation at the local level: transparency, vertical accountability, control of corruption, public administration procedures, and public service delivery. By this comparison, he concludes that anti-corruption and transparency are the most critical problems within Vietnam's one-party state.

In the fourth chapter, Abdul Malik shows that Indonesia's democratic government has difficulty in delivering substantive public goods, and ordinary citizens express their discontent in either violent or peaceful manner. According to him, this uneasy combination hinders government effectiveness and helps authoritarian nostalgia spread among citizens in Indonesia. He warns that both government and democracy in Indonesia are entering into a trap.

Turning to the second part of good government in Northeast Asia, three scholars conduct original research about the quality of government in Japan, China, and South Korea. The first of the three, Dr. Jou, investigates electoral mechanisms to make government responsive to citizens' ideological positions in Japan. His chapter focuses on policy representation, namely the degree to which individual opinions matched those of their government. Although many scholars agree that responsiveness is a necessary and desirable attribute of good government, empirical studies on representation have mostly focused on European and North American countries. Thus, Dr. Jou contributes to the literature by examining this important aspect of governance in the case of Japan through a longitudinal analysis of public opinions surveys. Specifically, he addresses the question of whether election results accurately reflect citizens' collective preferences, and he discusses both positive and negative conclusions regarding government accountability to the governed.

In the sixth chapter, Dr. Qi addresses a unique trust structure in China, inherited from Confucian tradition. Analyzing her original survey on local elections, she reports on China's persisting differential circles of trust in family members, relatives and friends, schoolmates, acquaintances, colleagues, and strangers. Her chapter shows that general trust in strangers does not perform differently in China than in Western countries, remaining positively associated with local governance. In China, the previously recognized "high-trust–low-government accountability" puzzle can be largely explained by the failure to differentiate Chinese particular trust from general trust measured by the standard trust question in surveys. In the chapter, Dr. Qi contributes to the literature by reexamining social capital and local governance in a Confucian society.

In the final and concluding chapter, Dr. Cho critically reviews recent efforts to evaluate the quality of government in both advanced and developing areas. He divides existing frameworks into minimalist and maximalist approaches and points out some limitations such as comparative utility, validity, and reliability. To respond to these limitations, he proposes a multidimensional framework, which can be applied to other developing countries, and analyzes how Koreans evaluate the quality of government. By analyzing results of a nationwide survey, he shows that a majority of Koreans evaluate their government's quality as problematic and evaluate procedural quality more negatively than outcome quality. He attributes this assessment to authoritarian modernization and flawed democracy after democratization. He suggests that the Korean government needs to improve procedural quality rather than outcome quality.

Overall, the six scholars in this book have reached the conclusion that corruption is the single most important problem within Asian governments. Whether their approaches are theoretical or empirical, the authors all agree that democratic institutions would help these countries improve the quality of government but their impacts are still limited, remaining at the embryonic stage, with the exception of Japan where electoral mechanisms help government follow citizens' political orientations. Furthermore, these scholars indicate explicitly and implicitly that overgrown government and its autonomous authority result in a gap between what government supplies and what the people demand, and Asian culture conditions this asymmetric relationship between government and civil society.

References

Charron, Nicholas, Lewis Dijkstra, and Victor Lapuente. 2015. "Mapping the Regional Divide in Europe: A Measure for Assessing Quality of Government in 206 European Regions." *Social Indicators Research* 122 (2): 315-346.

Fukuyama, Francis. 2011. *The Origins of Political Order: From Prehuman Times to the French Revolution.* New York: Farrar, Straus and Giroux.

———. 2014. *Political Order and Political Decay: From the Industrial Revolution to the Globalization of Democracy.* New York: Farrar, Straus and Giroux.

———. 2016. "Governance: What Do We Know, and How Do We Know It?" *Annual Review of Political Science* 19: 89-105.

Holmberg, Sören, Bo Rothstein, and Naghmeh Nasiritousi. 2009. "Quality of Government: What You Get." *Annual Review of Political Science* 12 (1): 135-161.

Huntington, Samuel P. 1968. *Political Order in Changing Societies.* New Haven, CT: Yale University Press.

Rothstein, Bo. 2011. *The Quality of Government: Corruption, Social Trust, and Inequality in International Perspective.* Chicago: University of Chicago Press.

Putnam, Robert. 1993. *Making Democracy Work.* Princeton: Princeton University Press.

Part 1

Good Government in Southeast Asia

2

Good Government in Malaysia: Issues, Challenges and Strategies in Combating Corruption

Benny Teh Cheng Guan
University of Science, Malaysia

Corruption is worse than prostitution. The latter might endanger the morals of an individual, the former invariably endangers the morals of the entire country.

Karl Kraus (1874–1936)

Introduction

The fundamental essence of good governance is the ability to make and implement good decisions. But for whom? Essentially, it is for the interests of the people. In short, good governance must have the people's well-being in mind. Doing so requires a government that is transparent in all its decision-making processes and is highly accountable to its people because decisions made are not to serve the powerful few but the community and society that it democratically represents.

Good government and good governance are prerequisites for a

country that upholds sustainable human development. In East Asia, however, they remain a problem. Yuriko Koike, a former defense minister and a current member of the Diet of Japan, recently wrote that "[t]he problems that are now bedeviling Burma, Malaysia, and Thailand may appear to have little in common. But they all spring from the same source: an entrenched elite's stubborn refusal to craft a viable system of governance that recognizes new and rising segments of society and reflects their interests in government policy" (Koike 2016).

Malaysia's rapid economic development, its integration into the international economic system, and the government's aim to support and encourage Internet literacy in the quest to build a knowledge economy and achieve its vision of becoming a developed country by 2020 have led to a segment of society represented by educated young adults who are not only Internet savvy but also critical of issues that affect the country, including those that epitomize bad governance such as corruption, inequitable distribution and wasteful spending. They are well informed and often turn to social media to vent their anger and dissatisfactions.

One issue that has taken center stage in recent times is corruption. Ernst & Young's Asia Pacific Fraud Survey for 2013 found that 39 percent of the respondents in Malaysia believe that corrupt practices are widespread in the country, a figure that nearly doubles the Asia Pacific average of 21 percent (Ernst & Young 2013, 18). Meanwhile, The Federation of Chinese Associations

Malaysia found from its survey at the end of 2013 that Malaysian Chinese have a high tolerance for graft (Woon 2013). A 2014 survey by CNBC and Burson-Marsteller found that *corruption* is the first word that comes to Malaysians' minds when they think of the government (*Malay Mail Online* 2014). *Foreign Policy* magazine lists Malaysia as one of the six worst corruption scandals of 2015 (O'Grady 2015). In the latest 2015 global Corruption Perceptions Index (CPI), Malaysia scored 5.0 and ranked 54 out of 168 countries surveyed, which suggests that it is an averagely corrupt country (see Table 1). The drop in ranking from 50 in 2014 to 54 in 2015 was due to allegations of corruption regarding a state-owned strategic investment company called 1MDB (1Malaysia Development Berhad) and the controversial donation of RM2.6 billion (US$666 million) that was found in Malaysian Prime Minister Najib Tun Razak's personal bank accounts (Carvalho 2016). Meanwhile, the Global Competitiveness Index (GCI) by the World Economic Forum ranks Malaysia at number 18 out of 140 countries and considers it to be the "highest ranked among the developing Asian economies" (Schwab 2015, 26). This may explain that whereas Malaysia's CPI ranking has hardly improved in the past ten years (see Table 1) and corruption continues to be a problem, it has not deteriorated to a level that would cause the loss of investor and business community confidence and adversely affect the country's ability to compete globally.

Table 1. **Corruption Perceptions Index (CPI) for Malaysia, 2006-2015**

Year	CPI Score	Rank
2006	5.0	44 (163)
2007	5.1	43 (180)
2008	5.1	47 (180)
2009	4.5	56 (180)
2010	4.4	56 (178)
2011	4.3	60 (183)
2012	4.9	54 (176)
2013	5.0	53 (177)
2014	5.2	50 (175)
2015	5.0	54 (168)

Source: Transparency International website (http://www.transparency.org).

Note: The CPI score is based on a scale from 0 to 10, with 0 for *highest perceived corruption* and 10 for *lowest perceived corruption.* Figure in parentheses ( ) represents the total number of countries surveyed.

This, however, is not to deny the possibility of a political crisis that could destabilize the country and confirm the prediction of political observers. Yuriko Koike wrote in the Project Syndicate in March 2015 that "[s]adly, Malaysia may soon become prone to the same type of violent protest and economic decline that have gripped Thailand in recent years. Here, it seems clear that UNMO's political interests have been allowed to dictate that the country's key opposition leader should be tried on charges that no real democracy that embraces the rule of law would even consider leveling, and convicted on evidence that no truly independent court would accept" (Koike 2015). Others such as Yang Razali Kassim, a senior fellow with the S. Rajaratnam School of International Studies in Singapore, have called the political situation a "mega crisis" (Kassim 2015).

Given that the issue of corruption is entangled with the problems of economic slowdown, prolonged depreciation of the Malaysian currency, and a leadership challenge that stands to not only affect national stability but also threatens the social fabric and peoples' well-being, this chapter employs a human security perspective by adopting a two-pronged top-down (protection) and bottom-up (empowerment) approach.[1] At the General Assembly of the United Nations Convention against Corruption in 2003, Secretary-General Ban Ki-Moon warned about the danger of corruption to human life when he said, "Corruption is an insidious plague It undermines democracy and the rule of law, leads to violations of human rights, distorts markets, erodes the quality of life, and allows organized crime, terrorism and other threats to...flourish Corruption hurts the poor disproportionately—by diverting funds intended for development, undermining a government's ability to provide basic services, feeding inequality and injustice, and discouraging foreign aid and investment (Ban 2003). In 2006, Paul Wolfowitz, then president of the World Bank, echoed a similar sentiment when he warned that "[t]oday one of the biggest threats to development in many countries... is corruption. It weakens

---

1 Under the concept of human security as espoused by the United Nations Development Program in 1994 and later refined in the 2003 "Human Security Now" report, the two approaches of top-down (focusing on the rule of law and institutions) and bottom-up (focusing on the empowerment of people) form the basic structure for analyzing issues that concern peoples' lives and interests. For more details on the concept, see Teh (2012).

fundamental systems, it distorts markets, and it encourages people to apply their skills and energies in nonproductive ways. In the end, governments and citizens will pay a price, a price in lower incomes [and] lower investment" (Wolfowitz 2006). Indeed, the link between corruption and human insecurities is well established (Tavanti and Stachowicz-Stanusch 2013). Corruption demoralizes human dignity, pervades different areas of peoples' lives and undoubtedly weakens governance. Good government is not simply vital in protecting people from the ill effects of corruption, but empowering them is necessary to ensure sustainable good governance.

The first of this chapter's five sections provides an understanding of the terms *good government* and *good governance* and contextualizes the problem of corruption in the country. The second section takes a top-down approach by examining the role of the government in devising policy initiatives and anti-corruption strategies in line with the notion of good government. The third section focuses on the bottom-up approach by analyzing the various activities organized by individuals and social movements aimed at voicing their disappointments, generating collective awareness, and empowering the people to seek redress for better governance. The discussions in sections 2 and 3 are contrasted with areas of contention highlighted and policy suggestions offered in the fourth section. The last section concludes the chapter.

Good Government, Good Governance, and the Problems of Corruption in Malaysia

Good government does not refer to the number of policies delivered but the quality of each of them on the basis of outcome indicators such as "low levels of corruption, prevalence of the rule of law, government effectiveness, or protection of property rights (Charron and Lapuente 2013, 567). A "good quality government would practice good public administration that is responsive, effective, efficient, and noncorrupt (H. Lim 2007, 34). The definition of *good government* can be further expanded to include characteristics such as political legitimacy of the ruling government, separation of powers, effective internal and external audit, low levels of corruption and nepotism, freedom of religion and movement, and the absence of arbitrary government power (Doig 1995, 151–152). It may also contain certain aspects deemed important to a particular country. Lourdesamy (2015) identified five characteristics of a good government that may be used as a reference for Malaysia: government powers must be clearly defined and limited; functions on democratic principles; must perform and produce results; is guided by fundamental values, principles, and morals; and respects diversity. Respecting differences is certainly an essential factor for a multicultural country like Malaysia.

No matter how the term *good government* is defined, the shared criterion is a "low level of corruption." As Alan Doig rightly points out, “no checklist of good government or good governance indicators would be either effective or workable with the pervasive and continuous use of money and influence to manipulate them (1995, 152). Focusing on the role of the government, *corruption* would refer to “the abuse of public roles or public power for private gain (Johnston 1998, 89). However, this definition alone is inadequate. It is necessary to ascertain that corruption is highly malignant and brings long-term detrimental effects to people and societies. For the purpose of this study, *good government* is therefore defined as a politically legitimate government that adheres to the separation of powers and puts in place effective top-down anticorruption strategies to root out abuses of public power without fear or favor to ensure that people’s interests and well-being are prioritized, respected and preserved.

The realization of good governance can only be made possible by the existence of good government. In short, good government is a necessary prerequisite for good governance (Doig 1995, 153). For the latter to be effective, not only do people’s interests need to be protected, but their participation in policy making must be highly encouraged and strongly supported. Whereas good government demonstrates a government’s ability to form good policy decisions, good governance demonstrates active participatory politics. *Good governance* is therefore defined as the practice of good policy decision making that actively involves the bottom-up participation of the populace and their empowerment to overcome threats and insecurities.

Corruption in Malaysia

Corruption involving politicians and bureaucrats in Malaysia has been in the limelight for many years. In the 1970s, Lim Kit Siang, an opposition member of parliament, alleged that corruption was visible especially among the higher-level officials (K. Lim 1978). Under the leadership of the fourth prime minister, Mahathir Mohamad, corruption was observed to have become a persistent concern with bureaucrats making up the majority of arrests, and corruption scandals involving ruling politicians were often reported (H. Lim 2002, 186). In one case involving a former Economic Planning Unit head, there were reports suggesting that Mahathir had interfered in the investigation process by ordering the then Anti-Corruption Agency (predecessor to the MACC) director, Shafee Yahaya, to close the case (Mokhtar 2015). This incident revealed the vulnerability of the agency and brought into question the seriousness of the Mahathir Administration in tackling graft. The numerous cases of corruption scandals since the early 1980s have, estimated a Morgan Stanley economist, caused the country to lose as much as US$100 billion (cited in *Malaysiakini* 2009).[2]

Furthermore, money politics have become a problem for "Malaysia Incorporated. As early as 1984, then-Prime Minister Mahathir Mohamad warned his party members at the 35th United Malays National Organization (UMNO) General Assembly

2 For details of some of the infamous scandals such as the Perwaja Steel and the Bumiputra Malaysia Finance cases, see *Malaysiakini* (2009).

that money politics, if left unchecked, would lead to the party's destruction (*Singapore Monitor* 1984).[3] Over the years, the situation spiraled downward and became so entrenched that he wept openly during UMNO's General Assembly in 1996 due to the "extent to which money politics had taken over his party (Musa 2001). Musa argues that Mahathir's "much ballyhooed Malaysia, Inc. concept, which envisions a collaborative partnership of public and private sectors, is in reality nothing but a camouflage for incestuous relationships between the party, government and business (2001). With his twenty-two years in office (1981–2003), critics believed that Mahathir could have done much more to eradicate corruption if he had been determined enough, although he did sack his then-Deputy Prime Minister Anwar Ibrahim over corruption and sodomy charges that the latter claimed was a political conspiracy.

When Abdullah Badawi became Malaysia's fifth prime minister, he emphasized the need to fight corruption and reiterated his determination and commitment to cleanse UMNO from graft (Case 2005). There were some successes. For example, the individual behind the infamous corruption case of Perwaja, Eric Chia, and a senator who was appointed as cabinet minister, Kasitah Gaddam, were charged in court for corruption (L. Lopez 2004). In addition, former chief minister of the state of Negeri Sembilan, Isa Samad, was suspended from UMNO for six years due to money politics, and his political secretary and a few other UMNO executive councillors were also suspended

3 UMNO is the dominant party in the current ruling coalition—the National Front.

for the same offense (Musa 2005). Among the cases involving civil servants was the case of former Kangar Municipal Council President Baharudin Ahmad, who was charged with four counts of corruption in 2004 (Soh 2004). Despite making some progress in fighting corruption, some individuals such as Anwar Ibrahim remained skeptical of Badawi, especially in regard to the involvement of his family members and close acquaintances in corruption, favoritism, or nepotism (George 2005).

When Najib Tun Razak replaced Abdullah Badawi as the sixth and current prime minister of Malaysia in April 2009, he embarked on a national transformation program to address a number of key concerns of the people. The results of the March 2008 general election showed that support for the ruling coalition had dropped drastically, and it was denied a two-thirds majority when only 63 percent of the seats were won, compared with 90 percent in the 2004 election. The Merdeka Center for Opinion Research carried out an opinion poll at the end of 2008 and found that corruption ranked as one of the leading concerns of the people (Merdeka Center 2009, 7). On the basis of further feedback from the public, fighting corruption was made one of the seven National Key Results Areas, reflecting the government's strong intention to improve its accountability.

Nevertheless, this intention has been overshadowed by a number of high-level political scandals such as the Port Klang Free Zone, National Feedlot Corporation, Scorpene submarines, and Ampang Light Rail Transit (LRT) tender, to name a few.[4] The latest news

---

4 For a long list of corruption-related cases that are based on news sources, see

that has gripped the nation is the 1MDB debacle involving serious accusations of corruption against the prime minister. An inquiry into the 1MDB's RM425 million (US$108 million) reported net profit by an opposition parliamentarian, Tony Pua, in 2010 (*Malaysia Today* 2010) and the subsequent reporting of 1MDB's accumulated debts of RM42 billion (US$10.7 billion) has eventually snowballed into a series of revelations by news portals such as *Sarawak Report*, British-based *The Sunday Times*, and *The Wall Street Journal* alleging corruption, money laundering, and cheating. The prime minister, Najib Tun Razak, who is the founder and also the head of the board of advisors of 1MDB, has been at the center of the controversy: He was accused of channeling RM2.6 billion (US$666 million) from 1MDB into his personal bank accounts. The Malaysian Anti-Corruption Commission (MACC) later confirmed from its investigations that the funds did not come from 1MDB (*Malay Mail Online* 2015). The head of Transparency International, Jose Ugaz, gave a bold speech at the 16th International Anti-Corruption Conference in Putrajaya, Malaysia, mentioning that [t]here are two questions that need to be answered. Who paid the money and why? Where did it go? One man could answer those questions. If that does not happen then only a fully independent investigation, free from political interference, can uncover the truth. Until that happens, no claim from the government on anti-corruption will be credible" (Ugaz 2015).

In January 2016, the Attorney-General cleared Najib Tun Razak of any wrongdoings, explaining that the funds were a personal

---

the Sinar Project website at http://accountable.sinarproject.org/issues.

donation from the Saudi royal family and concluding that the amount was not 'given corruptly' and was not used as 'inducement or reward' for Mr Najib to do anything in his capacity as Prime Minister (Teoh 2016).[5] This, however, has not stopped the opposition leaders and some ruling coalition members, including former Prime Minister Mahathir Mohamad and former Deputy Prime Minister Muhyiddin Yassin, to call for his resignation. In March 2016, political leaders and politicians from both sides of the political divide congregated in an unprecedented move in the political history of Malaysia and joined by civil society organizations (CSOs) and intellectuals to issue a Citizens' Declaration in support of the removal of the prime minister from office (*Malaysiakini* 2016a). With the 1MDB mired in controversy and still under international investigations by four countries—the United States, Singapore, Luxembourg, and Switzerland, the prime minister's approval ratings have dropped to an all-time low of 23 percent (Finance Twitter 2015). Unsatisfied with the attorney-general's decision to acquit the prime minister, the Malaysian Bar passed a motion at its Annual General Meeting in March 2016 calling for his resignation; Mahathir Mohamad and two other individuals initiated a lawsuit against the prime minister for "corruption and misfeasance in public office" in the same month (Holmes 2016; Naidu 2016).

5 It was further reported that 91 percent of the funds were returned but no explanations were provided on why the donation was given and what the remaining 9 percent was used for (Teoh 2016).

Policy Initiatives, Programs, and Anti-Corruption Strategies

Since independence in 1957, Malaysia has, over time, employed and refined to a certain extent several anti-corruption strategies to combat corruption at home. This section briefly discusses the roles played by laws, programs, and key formal institutions, namely the MACC, the Public Complaints Bureau (PCB), the Ombudsman, the Parliament, and the Public Accounts Committee (PAC), in augmenting public accountability and hence good governance.

The history of the MACC can be traced back to 1961 when the Prevention of Corruption Act was established. In 1967, the government created an Anti-Corruption Agency (ACA) under the purview of the prime minister's department to overcome malpractices and eliminate corruption. The Prevention of Corruption Act was repealed in 1997 and replaced with the Anti-Corruption Act. Over the years, the ACA suffered from a credibility crisis as people doubted its independence. After frequent calls from the public and lobbying from interest groups, the Badawi administration showed political will when the 1997 act was repealed and replaced with the Malaysian Anti-Corruption Commission Act in 2009, effectively establishing the MACC. It was modeled after anti-corruption agencies in Hong Kong and Australia and was designed to be an independent and transparent body.

The functions of the MACC are listed under Section 7 of the

MACC Act 2009 (MACC website: www.sprm.gov.my) as follows:

- To receive and consider any report of the commission of an offence under this Act and to investigate such reports.
- To detect and investigate any suspected offence or attempt or conspiracy to commit any offence under the MACC Act 2009.
- To examine the practices, systems and procedures of public bodies in order to facilitate the discovery of offences under the MACC Act 2009.
- To instruct, advise, and assist any person on ways in which corruption may be eliminated.
- To advise heads of public bodies of any changes in practices, systems, or procedures to reduce the likelihood of the occurrence of corruption.
- To educate the public against corruption.
- To enlist and foster public support against corruption.

Its aims are therefore to educate, to prevent, and to investigate. In an effort to gain the confidence, trust, and credibility of the people, the MACC's performance is monitored by five independent bodies that represent the general public, namely the Anti-Corruption Advisory Board, Special Committee on Corruption, Complaints Committee, Operations Review Panel, and Consultation and Corruption Prevention Panel (ibid).[6] In addition to the MACC, a Malaysian Anti-Corruption Academy was set up to offer courses and training to government

---

6 These bodies comprise "ex-government officials, politicians (government and opposition), professionals from the business and corporate sectors, academicians, lawyers, and well respected individuals" (ibid.).

officers including individuals from other Asian countries.[7]

As mentioned earlier, Prime Minister Najib Tun Razak spearheaded an innovative program called the Government Transformation Program (GTP) to improve government accountability, and one of the seven National Key Results Areas is to fight corruption. Among the initiatives identified were to enhance enforcement agencies, combat grand corruption, transform the auditor-general's reporting process, further enhance the government procurement process, and raise public support and enhance public education (Pemandu website: https://www.pemandu.gov.my). The 2014 Annual Report of the GTP showed that several actions have been taken by the government. In 2010, the Whistleblower Protection Act was introduced to encourage individuals to report evidence of corruption. The report indicated that 392 individuals have been given protection under the act (Pemandu 2014, 170).[8] In 2011, Special Corruption Sessions Courts were implemented throughout the country to clear the backlog and expedite corruption cases (ibid., 155). The idea of incorporating an anti-corruption syllabus in primary and secondary schools' textbooks was also mooted to sow good ethical habits (ibid., 165).

Numerous initiatives have also been taken to enhance the operations, human capital, and prevention measures against corruption.

---

7 Apart from its various courses, it also offers an accredited master's degree program in corruption studies.

8 This act is complemented by the Witness Protection Act 2009 that aims to protect witnesses of corruption cases who may fear for their safety.

Some of them include the MACC team-based investigation method, the PEACE interview method, and the setting up of a video interviewing room (Pemandu 2014, 163). A "name and shame database of corruption offenders has also been created and is accessible online. On anti-corruption awareness campaigns, the MACC has been playing a proactive role, and one of the activities carried out was the setting up of an Anti-Corruption Secretariat in universities to raise awareness of the dangers of corrupt practices and to obtain the support of young adults as "ambassadors in spreading the message to others. The government is expected to soon present in Parliament a draft of the Corporate Liability Provision for insertion into the MACC Act that will hold corporations "liable for directly or indirectly encouraging its employees to engage in corrupt practices (ibid, 162).

Akin to the MACC, another "executive-controlled mechanism for bureaucratic accountability" (quoted in H. Lim 2002, 178) is the aforementioned PCB. The objectives of the PCB, among others, are to "resolve complaints efficiently, fairly, and effectively as promised in the PCB Client's Charter, improve the rate of resolving complaints received from the public, provide and improve facilities for the public to lodge complaints, and reduce repetitive complaints against the public services (PCB website: www.pcb.gov.my). Housed under the Prime Minister's Department, the PCB's powers, support, and resources and hence its efficacy are dependent on the government (H. Lim 2002, 179). Calls for an independent ombudsman were rejected in 1968 in lieu of the PCB. When the ombudsman idea was broached in 2010 through an open letter by a concerned citizen, the director-general of the PCB insisted that the PCB's "direct relationship with other government agencies" would it give an advantage over the ombudsman in seeing "through [its] recommendations or resolutions of complaints" (Tam 2010).

The parliament is not only a place to debate and pass laws but plays a vital role in overseeing the actions and checking the powers of the executive branch. Because it consists of lawmakers democratically elected by the people, it therefore represents the interests of the citizens and has the legislative power to hold government institutions accountable. In reality, this is proving harder to achieve. Although Malaysia practices a parliamentary system with constitutional monarchy, the role of the parliament has declined and weakened over the years. Shad Saleem Faruqi, an emeritus professor of law, commented in a local newspaper that the parliament is not legislating but merely legitimating due to the dominant role of the executive (Faruqi 2015). One explanation for its increased dominance in parliament is the ability of the ruling coalition, the National Front, to maintain its majority in most of the nation's general elections. The executive has been able to turn the parliament into its subservient arm and has succeeded in removing "constitutional constraints and passed laws that expand its powers and discretion in relation to society" (K. Lim 2002, 181).

The role of the opposition in providing checks and balances has been particularly weak. However, the opposition parties were able to regain some of their strengths in parliament when they succeeded in making further inroads in the last (thirteenth) general election in

2013 by reducing the ruling coalition's share to a simple majority. A stronger opposition would definitely provide better checks and balances, especially in efforts to combat corruption.

The PAC, a standing committee of the lower house of parliament and made up of members from the ruling and opposition parties, is equally significant in combating graft because it is one of the key instruments of parliamentary scrutiny. The purpose of the PAC is to promote a culture of accountability in which it ensures ex post supervision of the financial management process (Ofosu-Amaah et al. 1999). More specifically, the PAC "examines public accounts and responds to the Auditor-General's reports on issues involving the misappropriation of public funds, and government inefficiency and/or ineffectiveness and "has the power to summon witnesses and demand documents and information necessary for its investigations (Saleh and Abu Hasan 2015, 215, 218). The auditor-general's responsibility is to audit and report to the parliament on the financial management of government agencies. It is hence in a position to raise and highlight any possibilities of extravagance, discrepancies, and corrupt practices pertaining to public spending. Thus, the PAC works closely with the auditor-general's office.

In recent years, the PAC has provided its input on various cases including controversial issues such as the National Feedlot Corporation and the Port Klang Free Zone. In the former, the PAC revealed that there was mismanagement of the National Feedlot Corporation in achieving its target on annual beef production set by the government (*The Star* 2014). It also highlighted that there were some major flaws in the standard operating procedures of the Ministry of Agriculture and Agro-Based Industry and the Ministry of Finance in the awarding and disbursing of funds to the National Feedlot Corporation. In the latter, the PAC's investigations found that there were possible abuses of power and called upon the former transport minister and former general manager of the Port Klang Authority to be investigated for criminal breach of trust (*Bernama* 2009).

The Role of Civil Society Movements in Fighting Corruption

The bottom-up process is equally, if not more, important in voicing concerns and creating awareness when there are possible abuses of power and squandering of resources that could adversely affect people's interests or worse, threaten their freedom from fear and freedom from want.[9] As aptly captured by the former vice chairman of Transparency International, Tunku Abdul Aziz, "It is worth reminding ourselves at the outset that no matter how we define it, corruption exacts a heavy toll on a nation's political, social and economic development, and the victims, as always, are the poorest,

9 "Freedom from fear" refers to the protection from immediate harmful acts such as physical violence, torture, political oppression, and abuse, whereas "freedom from want" refers to the safety from less traumatic acts such as pandemics, poverty, hunger, access to clean water, discrimination, and natural disasters that equally affect the survival of individuals (see Teh 2012).

the marginalised and the least educated members of our society" (Abdul Aziz n.d).[10]

Raising Awareness through Social Media

Civil society organizations can play a crucial role in building collective awareness of corrupt practices and stir citizens to voice their dissatisfaction through nonviolent methods such as protests, petitions, marches, sit-ins, vigils, public speeches, and political rallies as well as the use of evolving social networking technologies such as Facebook, Twitter, Instagram, and blogs to monitor public spending, share news reports, and exchange views on the latest developments in the country. There have been numerous cases of nonviolent civil disobedience and civil resistance around the world from Gandhi to the Rose and Orange revolutions (see Roberts and Ash 2009). When people realize the civil power that they command and are mobilized in huge numbers, they form a social force that is capable of demanding justice and accountability from their governments. The significance of people power lies in its ability to "disrupt or shake-up the system itself, making it more difficult for the corruption to continue as normal and supporting the honest people within the corrupt system who want to change it" (New Tactics 2010). External pressures are beneficial when corruption has crept deep into the system and become well entrenched, and there is

---

10 Transparency International is a CSO based in Berlin and has more than 100 national chapters, including one in Malaysia.

a severe lack of political will to root it out due to too many vested interests keen on preserving the status quo.

In Malaysia, alternative media such as *Malaysiakini*, *Malaysia Today*, *Free Malaysia Today*, and *The Malaysian Insider* have sought to take advantage of the Internet to provide alternative views that may not be reported or covered by the mainstream media. The power of the Internet lies not only in its capability to permit real-time information to flow freely across spatial and temporal boundaries but also in its capacity to allow alternative media to circumvent authoritative governments in providing an alternative source of information compared with traditional media that some have found to be too government friendly. Mustafa Anuar, then a lecturer of communication studies, analyzed the reporting of the mainstream media on the 2004 general election in Malaysia and observed that "the Malaysian press overwhelmingly presented a sympathetic, and often flaunting, bias in favor of the incumbent BN [ruling coalition] while providing insufficient coverage of the views of—or even demonizing—the opposition parties" (Anuar 2005, 25).

The success of the alternative media in wooing Malaysian readers and followers, according to Steven Gan, cofounder and editor-in-chief of *Malaysiakini*, was due to the government's pledge not to censor the Internet, the rise in political conscience among the people, and the loss of credibility of the mainstream media caused by self-censorship (Gan 2002). The Internet provided not only the space for the growth of alternative media reporting but also an avenue for opposition parties frustrated by insufficient news coverage of their views to deliver their viewpoints directly to readers, and a platform for political bloggers to pitch their ideas on issues of governance and moral values. Jeff Ooi, a blogger-turned-politician, for example, used his blog to discuss issues related to corruption and mismanagement of public funds (Theophilus 2008). Information and discussions generated through blogs, Facebook, and news portals help enhance people's level of awareness on issues that affect them. Informed netizens can then act as catalysts in enriching off-line discussions with family members and friends. The significance of social media was recognized when five of the six bloggers who ran in the 2008 general election actually won. Even then-Prime Minister Abdullah Badawi had to concede that social media has influence in Malaysian politics. He was quoted as saying that [w]e didn't think it was important. It was a serious misjudgment. We thought that the newspapers, the print media, the television were important but young people were looking at text messages and blogs" (*New Straits Times* 2008).

To be certain, Malaysian online news media are not the only source of alternative information. Once online, Malaysians have access to foreign media reporting as well. On the 1MDB issue, for example, *Sarawak Report* and *The Wall Street Journal* have provided readers with numerous alternative news articles, which were then widely picked up by local and foreign news portals. The allegations they raised have earned them the wrath of the Najib administration, with the prime minister mulling over the decision to sue them for defamation.

Speaking Out through Creative Means and Nonviolent Protests

In 2014, Transparency International produced an anti-corruption kit containing 15 ideas for young activists. The ideas were categorized into four themes: "Keep Watch," "Get Creative," "Mobilize," and "Make Elections Count" (Goudie, Burnett, and Thayenthal 2014). Blogs and other forms of social media where information and ideas are shared and exchanged allow online communities and networks to "keep watch" on issues concerning the people. They are also useful in providing feedback to governments on public services matters. However, social media has limitations because it excludes those who are not netizens. Town hall–style public gatherings remain essential especially when they are able to generate media attention and prompt responses from the government. In Penang state, for example, the Penang Forum, made up of an informal network of Penang-based CSOs and concerned individuals, occasionally organizes public forums to discuss important issues such as local elections, transport plans, or hillside developments that would then be highlighted to the local and state governments in the quest of developing a more participatory structure of governance. The Forum empowers individuals to raise their concerns and/or offer suggestions. Many other CSOs in the country such as the Center to Combat Corruption and Cronyism play similar roles in keeping watch and empowering the people through projects and events. The next two subsections take a closer look at several bottom-up ideas under the categories of "Get Creative" and "Mobilize."

Get Creative—Comics and Cartoons

There are obviously various creative ways individuals can express their opinions. One method is through the use of funny images and text. Comics and cartoons can illustrate people's daily lives and struggles in a humorous way yet carry certain political or social predispositions. In Malaysia, there are a number of well-known artists including Mohammad Nor Khalid (better known by his pen name Lat), C. W. Kee, Zulkiflee Anwar Ulhaque (who goes by his pen name Zunar), and Fahmi Reza.

Lat's work dates back to the 1970s; his satirical pieces depicted the scenes of everyday life and social changes that came with economic development and urbanization. He showed Malaysia as a multicultural society with its own traditions and brought to light issues of national identity. He has also been critical of politicians, portraying them in exaggerated ways but without malicious intent. According to Muliyadi Mahamood, "the most important factor of Lat's popularity is that through his humor, he manages to poke fun at the flaws of society and the government and criticize them in a subtle way" (2014, 207). His art projects "another reality that is a counterweight to the official regime established by the highest levels in Malaysia… [and] serves as an educational tool… [that] can ignite a social consciousness that can potentially bring changes for future generations" (Abella and Reyes 2014, 13). Conferred the Fukuoka Prize for Arts and Culture in 2002, Lat summed up his role as follows: "I believe the purpose of drawing cartoons and providing commentary is to be positive. In other words, anything you say should at its core be honest and sincere. Cartoonists should not try to bring down anybody or promote anybody—for example, politicians. We all need to laugh and have fun, and this is what I hope to provide through my cartoons" (Lat 2002, 11).

Another cartoonist who paints the everyday scenes of Malaysian life is C. W. Kee. His comic appears daily in the local mainstream newspaper *The Star* and touches more on social and economic issues that involve people's idiosyncrasies, selfishness, or inconsiderate behaviors than on particular political figures. Unlike Kee and Lat, whose cartoons are more social commentary shedding light on Malaysian society, Zunar's sketches are particularly critical of the political establishment. He has steadfastly pushed the political boundaries and ventured into areas that most cartoonists would choose to avoid, poking fun at sensitive contemporary issues such as corruption, race, religion, the judiciary system, nepotism, the 1MDB, and even the prime minister and his wife. His work aims to "punch" rather than "pinch" to ensure that the message he intends to convey reaches his readers loud and clear (Soon 2010). He has been considered by observers to wear a few hats as "a political cartoonist, a political analyst, a freedom fighter, and a visionary" (ibid.). As such, his drawings have elicited the ire of the present government. His cartoon books were banned by the Home Ministry in 2010, but he succeeded in challenging the ministry's decision in the court of appeal: The judges found no evidence of the books being a threat to public order (*The Sun Daily* 2014). He has also been arrested and charged with sedition twice, once in 2010 and again in 2015, the latter for which he is awaiting trial.

Perhaps in a similar vein to Zunar, Fahmi Reza uses art to express his outrage and take a stand on issues of bad governance that have affected the country. He belongs to a group of rebel artists who call themselves Graphic Rebel for Protest & Activism. Not a true cartoonist, Reza recently depicted Prime Minister Najib Tun Razak as an "evil clown" online, and he was reprimanded by the Police Cyber Investigation Response Center for his action. It did not stop him but instead emboldened him to push the boundaries further. He was quoted in Aljazeera as saying, "I hope that my defiance and disobedience against authority will inspire others to do the same. People need to have the courage to stand up against injustice, against corruption… I am not afraid of being detained for speaking up. I believe that in a country where artists and satirists have been censored, arrested and incarcerated for their art, it is important that this form of artistic expression—parody and satire as a form of political protest—continues to be practiced and defended at all costs" (Mayberry 2016).

Mobilize—Petitions and Protests

Declarations, petitions, and peaceful protests or rallies are ways to build momentum and mobilize the masses to join forces in publicly displaying their discontentment with important issues that threaten their well-being, such as corruption and the suppression of freedom of expression. The Citizens' Declaration is one example. *Malaysiakini*'s opinion poll found that more than three fourths of the respondents supported the declaration (*Malaysiakini* 2016b). An online petition in support of the declaration to oust the current prime minister and restore the integrity of key institutions was set up in Change.org and had collected 51,589 signatures as of April 25, 2016 (Khalib 2016). Petitions can indeed be effective in empowering individuals to seek support from the public for a particular issue. In the United Kingdom, a group of Malaysian students studying at Nottingham University used a petition to raise support for their idea to present a motion on whether the Malaysian Society of the university should lobby the university to take down a two-meter-high portrait of Najib Tun Razak as an expression of collective disagreement for how the issue of the RM2.6 billion was handled (Chung 2016).[11]

Malaysians have also taken their grumbling and disappointments to the streets to express their dissatisfactions through organized rallies and protests. The sacking of Anwar Ibrahim as the deputy prime minister in 1998 and his subsequent arrest led to the mobilization of massive protests, with chants of *reformasi* (reformation) and demands for his release and an end to corruption and cronyism. The protests consisted of civil disobedience, sit-ins, marches, and even online activism and reflected a higher level of awareness among the people about the problems of governance that were transpiring at that time.

---

11 Although the petition sought 100 signatures, it garnered close to 5,000. The motion was accepted and debated at the Malaysian Society's annual general meeting but was defeated by an overwhelming majority.

A series of mass demonstrations were held in 2007, 2011, 2012, and 2015 by a coalition of CSOs called *Bersih* ("clean" in Malay), and at times in cooperation with opposition parties, demanding fair and clean elections. At the second *Bersih* rally in 2011, the organizer expanded the four unfulfilled demands of 2007's rally to eight points, including an end to corruption.[12] The 2015 *Bersih* rally was billed as an anti-corruption drive that saw a huge turnout—the organizer estimated there were 200,000 people, whereas the police provided a figure of 30,000—and the two-day protest was reported as orderly and calm (*The Economist* 2015). The members of Graphic Rebel for Protest & Activism lent their expertise by creating more than a hundred placards for protesters to download and print. With allegations of corruption in government, the protesters demanded, among other things, a clean government, improvement of the economy, and the resignation of the prime minister. Unlike previous rallies, this one received support from the Malaysian diaspora in fifty cities around the world who showed their solidarity with the protesters in the country. *Bersih* received international acclaim for its role in pushing for electoral reform when it was chosen as the co-recipient of South Korea's 2016 Gwangju Prize for Human Rights (*Malay Mail Online* 2016).[13] Apart from the *Bersih* rallies, there

---

12 The eight points were cleansing of the electoral roll, use of indelible ink, reform of postal voting, a minimum campaign period of twenty-one days, strengthening of public institutions, free and fair access to the mainstream media, ending of "dirty politics," and ending of corruption.

13 The Gwangju Prize is established by The May 18 Memorial Foundation and is given to individuals or organizations in recognition of their contributions

were other street protests focusing on issues such as the allegations of vote buying and vote rigging in the 2013 general election, the disagreement over the implementation of the goods and services tax, and the environmental and health concerns about the establishment of a rare-earth refinery.

Contentions between Top-down and Bottom-up Approaches and the Way Forward

Despite government efforts to introduce anti-corruption policies, campaigns, and programs to address the problem of corruption and money politics in the country, other stakeholders such as the alternative media, CSOs, opposition parties, individuals, and even several ruling coalition members have grown increasingly wary of the lack of accountability, as observed from their many activities aimed at pushing for a better government and governance. References were at times made to the auditor-general's annual reports as a key source of evaluating the government's level of accountability in managing public funds. The reports have in the recent past identified wasteful spending and mismanagement by government agencies (Gangopadhyay 2013).

The MACC, an anti-corruption strategy of the government, has

to the promotion of democracy, peace and human rights in their respective communities.

seen its success rate grow from 54 percent in 2009 to around 80 percent in 2015 (MACC 2015). But although the conviction rate of corruption cases has surpassed international standards, public perception of corruption in the country has hardly improved, as indicated by the CPI. This is likely due to the perceived problem of high-powered corruption cases remaining largely unresolved and the continued lax attitude of the people toward corruption. Greg Lopez, a research fellow at Murdoch University, opined that meaningful anti-corruption reforms are impossible because the MACC is not an independent body and the majority of the people have yet to change their attitude toward patronage and corruption (G. Lopez 2015).

Nonetheless, *Bersih*'s efforts in protesting for electoral reforms, for example, have, according to Ambiga Sreenevasan, co-chair of the 2011 *Bersih* rally, "made inroads in raising public awareness… [and] the resulting public pressure has forced the federal government and the election commission to take a position on these issues and to make some overtures—albeit not entirely satisfactory—towards electoral reform" (Sreenevasan 2013). The Najib administration announced in August 2011 that the government would set up a parliamentary select committee on electoral reforms. The committee, upon feedback from public hearings, formulated twenty-two recommendations in April 2012, but *Bersih* found a few drawbacks, questioning "whether the existing Election Commission has sufficient credibility to commit itself to undertaking the proposed recommendations" (Bersih 2.0 2012).

The government does not take civil disobedience lightly and

often resorts to laws such as the Sedition Act and the Peaceful Assembly Act for punishment. These laws have been criticized and viewed as problematic. The Sedition Act, originally enacted under the British colonial authority in 1948 and considered by Malaysia's Human Rights Commission as not fully in compliance with "international norms on the right to freedom of expression and speech," has been actively used to detain individuals deemed as seditious (SUHAKAM 2015, 14). Suara Rakyat Malaysia (SUARAM), a CSO that monitors and advocates for human rights in Malaysia, showed in its latest report that the number of people—ranging from elected representatives to activists and academics—being investigated, charged, or convicted in 2013, 2014, and 2015 were eighteen, forty-four, and 220, respectively (2015, 16). The opposition and some CSOs have purported that the act is being used to silence dissent. Meanwhile, the Peaceful Assembly Act, which has been used to arrest rally organizers for failure to notify the police ten days before their events, prohibits the participation of individuals under 15 years old and is thus considered to go against Article 15 of the United Nations Convention on the Rights of the Child, which acknowledges children's right to peaceful assembly (SUHAKAM 2013, 106).[14] There have also been concerns about the use of tear gas, water cannons, and alleged police brutality against protesters at rallies such as those organized by *Bersih* (Palani 2012).

Information and allegations from alternative sources on corrupt

14 Malaysia has been a state party to the United Nations Convention on the Rights of the Child since 1995.

practices have likewise put the government in a defensive mode. Internet access to the *Sarawak Report*, the Hong Kong–based *Asia Sentinel*, and The Malaysian Insider website in Malaysia has been blocked by the government in the past. The latter finally ceased its operations in March 2016 after Editor Jahabar Sadiq claimed that the website had suffered from months of pressure from the government to dissuade state-owned enterprises from advertising with it (*The Guardian* 2016). In July last year, the Edge Media Group, which owns The Malaysian Insider, received a three-month suspension order from the Home Ministry for the publishing permit of its two financial newspapers—the *Edge Weekly* and the *Edge Financial Daily*. The reason provided was that their reports on the 1MDB issue were "prejudicial or likely to be prejudicial to public order, security or likely to alarm public opinion or is likely to be prejudicial to public and national interest" (quoted in Ram 2015). The government's "move to shut us down in order to shut us up," as stated by the group's CEO Ho Kay Tat, has been criticized as inappropriate by a number of stakeholders, namely the National Union of Journalists Malaysia, the chairman of CIMB Group who is also the brother of Prime Minister Najib Tun Razak, the chief executive of AirAsia, the former International Trade and Industry minister, *Malaysiakini*, the Center for Independent Journalism Malaysia, the Foreign Correspondents Club of Malaysia, and the youth chief of an opposition party (ibid.). The contention between the government and the other stakeholders over this matter reflects differences in perceptions and priorities. Whereas the former sees critical reporting of the government as a threat to political stability and even national security, the latter believe restraining criticisms runs contrary to the spirit of freedom of the press and the concept of good government.

What Needs to Be Done?

The most urgent and effective measure to show the government's resolve in upholding the principles of transparency and accountability as well as to pledge zero tolerance on graft is to empower the MACC by making it a fully independent body that aptly reflects its principles of "independent, transparent and professional" and provide it with the power to prosecute. The MACC should therefore be placed under the scrutiny of the parliament. Given that the Corruption Eradication Commission in Indonesia has had prosecutorial powers since its establishment in 2003, the Malaysian Parliamentary Select Committee on Corruption has proposed to give the MACC the power to prosecute on two occasions but, unfortunately, these were rejected (Transparency International-Malaysia 2014). A special report of Transparency International's Malaysian chapter noted that the power to prosecute is important because "[w]hile the [MACC] has power to initiate investigations and to recommend prosecution, the final decision to charge rests with the Attorney-General, who is perceived to be highly susceptible to influence from his political masters" (Yoon 2003). In July 2015, the prime minister decided to remove Attorney-General Abdul Gani Patail and his Deputy Prime Minister Muhyiddin Yassin in what political analysts and observers saw as an attempt to interfere in the investigation process surrounding the 1MDB issue (*Channel News Asia* 2015). Concerned by the political developments in the country, Yassin took to social media in February 2016 to warn that the country was heading toward a dictatorship (Parameswaran 2016).

Other key institutions, especially the PCB, the judiciary, and the electoral system, need to be reformed to strengthen their roles in stopping corruption. Since the government has decided against the idea of an ombudsman, it should seriously consider empowering the PCB by safeguarding its independence and impartiality. Even though statistics showed that the percentage of cases resolved for the past three years (2013, 2014, and 2015) were more than 95 percent,[15] the fact that it is part of the government machinery may arguably deter some individuals from lodging complaints. Even more imperative is the preservation of an independent and competent court system to ensure that judges are impartial in dispensing their duties and the punishment commensurate with the severity of the crime. The court's 2015 sentencing of Mohamad Khir Toyo, a former chief minister of a wealthy state in Malaysia, for a property-related graft involving RM6.5 million (US$1.6 million) of only one year in prison and subsequent release on parole after six months could send the wrong message to the public

15 For details, see http://www.pcb.gov.my/en/complaint/statistics-by-year.

that “crime does pay (Mokhtar 2016). Equally, it is befitting that the electoral system must be clean and fair because an election empowers the populace in a democratic country to reject patronage and corruption through the casting of their votes. Allegations of gerrymandering and the lack of accountability of the Election Commission have generated immense public attention and street protests.

In addition, the strong political business ties that have enabled funds to be raised to “finance political ascendancy” in internal party, state, or general elections need to be dismantled because they breed nepotism and cronyism (Gomez 2005, 226). Overcoming corruption in party financing such as in UMNO, whereby the amount of funds used in UMNO’s elections substantially surpassed the sum used for general election campaigns, ultimately requires political will (ibid., 219). The Corporate Liability Provision draft, if approved, would be a significant move in the right direction.

Furthermore, stronger efforts ought to be taken in cultivating a robust relationship between government agencies and other stakeholders, if all parties are indeed on the same page in ridding the country of corruption. Restricting people’s freedom of expression and speech, and arresting and punishing individuals for voicing their concerns on fraud and graft are counterproductive and jeopardize the sanctity of democratic values as enshrined in the country’s constitution. The government’s commitment to free the country of corruption is not only to its population but also to the international community. Malaysia has, after all, been a state party to the United Nations Convention against Corruption since 2008.

Conclusion

A good government is a government that is committed to the independence and integrity of top-down institutions tasked to combat corruption, provides ample spaces for its citizens to voice their frustrations, and is always prepared to engage concerned communities in honest partnerships and consultations. In other words, a good government is a government that strives to dismantle the concentration of powers and is not egotistical with regard to sharing those powers with other stakeholders irrespective of their political leanings, therefore reconfiguring a typical traditional hierarchical structure of governance into a more equitable horizontal structure that celebrates participatory governance.

Although the government has a number of anti-corruption institutions and programs in place, their lack of independence and transparency have caused them to suffer from accountability and be perceived as tools for political manipulation. This has caused Malaysians to grow wary of their effectiveness in dealing with serious allegations of corruption involving office bearers who are entrusted to protect people's interests and well-being. With limited space to defy the authorities, individuals, civil society movements, and opposition parties increasingly turn to the Internet and use social media as platforms to generate awareness and raise public support on corruption-related issues. Bolder individuals have utilized their talents through their mighty pen or brush to push the political limits of acceptable behavior in order to disrupt the system and seek change. This includes whistle-blowers and witnesses who brave the risk in serving the public good.

As long as tensions between the top-down and bottom-up approaches persist, anti-corruption efforts would yield meaningless results. For convergence to occur, anti-corruption institutions need to be 100-percent free from political interference, and citizens need to cultivate a strong civic sense that will categorically reject pork-barreling, cronyism, nepotism, illegal rent-seeking, and corruption.

References

Abdul Aziz, Tunku. n.d. "Civil Society and the Fight against Corruption: Some Malaysian Civil Society Initiatives." Accessed April 11, 2016. http://unpan1.un.org/intradoc/groups/public/documents/apcity/unpan002897.pdf.

Abella, Mireya Sosa, and Ricardo Mariano Reyes. 2014. "Political Humor in Comic Strips: A Comparative Analysis between Oriental and Occidental Approaches." *International Journal of Cultural Studies* 1–18.

Anuar, Mustafa K. 2005. "Politics and the Media in Malaysia." *Kasarinlan: Philippine Journal of Third World Studies* 20 (1): 25–47.

Ban, Ki-moon. 2003. Secretary-General's Statement on the Adoption by the General Assembly of the United Nations Convention against Corruption. October 31. Accessed April 8, 2016. http://www.un.org/sg/statements/?nid=602.

Bernama. 2009. "PKFZ: PAC Wants Chan Kong Choy, OC Phang Investigated for CBT." November 4.

Bersih 2.0. 2012. "Response from Bersih 2.0 to the Recommendations of the Parliamentary Select Committee on Electoral Reform." April 3. Accessed April 14, 2016. http://www.bersih.org/response-from-bersih-2-0-to-the-recommendations-of-the-parliamentary-select-committee-on-electoral-reform/.

Carvalho, Martin. 2016. "Malaysia Slides Four Points down Global Corruption Perception Index." *The Star*, January 27.

Case, William. 2005. "Abdullah Badawi's First Year as Malaysia's Prime Minister." Regional Outlook Paper No. 2, Griffith Asia Institute.

Channel News Asia. 2015. "Removal of Malaysia's DPM and AG Seen as 'Acts of Desperation': Analysts." July 28.

Charron, Nicholas, and Lapuente, Victor. 2013. "Why Do Some Regions in Europe Have a Higher Quality of Government?" *The Journal of Politics* 75 (3): 567–582.

Chung, Cassandra. 2016. "Removing Dato' Seri Najib Razak's Portrait off the University of Nottingham." Accessed April 13, 2016. https://www.change.org/p/university-of-nottingham-removing-dato-seri-najib-razak-s-portrait-at-the-university-of-nottingham.

Doig, Alan. 1995. "Good Government and Sustainable Anti-Corruption Strategies: A Role for Independent Anti-Corruption Agencies?" *Public Administration and Development* 15 (2): 151–165.

Ernst & Young. 2013. *Building a More Ethical Business Environment: Asia-Pacific Fraud Survey 2013*. Ernst & Young Global Limited.

Faruqi, Shad Saleem. 2015. "Parliament's Constitutional Role." *The Star*, March 19.

Finance Twitter. 2015. "Uh-oh, Najib in Trouble—Get Ready for a Snap Election Next Year 2016." October 18. Accessed April 14, 2016. http://www.financetwitter.com/2015/10/uh-oh-najib-in-trouble-get-ready-for-a-snap-election-next-year-2016.html.

Gan, Steven. 2002. "Virtual Democracy in Malaysia." *Nieman Reports*, June 15.

Gangopadhyay, Abhrajit. 2013. "Malaysia Auditors Accuse Government of Wasteful Spending." *The Wall Street Journal*, October 3.

George, K. 2005. "Corruption Spreads Its Ugly Wings." *Aliran Monthly* 25 (3).

Gomez, Edmund Terence. 2005. "The State, Governance, and Corruption in Malaysia." In *Corruption and Good Governance in Asia*, edited by Nicholas Tarling. London: Routledge, 214–244.

Goudie, Yvonne, Stephanie Burnett, and Anna Thayenthal. 2014. *Anti-Corruption Kit: 15 Ideas for Young Activists*. Berlin: Transparency International.

Holmes, Oliver. 2016. "Former Malaysian Premier Mahathir Sues PM Najib over 'Abuse of Power.'" *The Guardian*, March 23.

Johnston Michael. 1998. "Fighting Systemic Corruption: Social Foundations for Institutional Reform." In *Corruption and Development*, edited by Mark Robinson. London: Frank Cass Publishers, 85–104.

Kassim, Yang Razali. 2015. "Najib and Malaysian Politics in Crisis: Whither UMNO and the Opposition?" S. Rajaratnam School of International Studies (RSIS) Commentaries, July 30.

Khalib, Azrul Mohd. 2016. "Quit! Undur!" Petitioning Prime Minister of Malaysia Dato' Seri @NajibRazak. Accessed April 13, 2016. https://www.change.org/p/prime-minister-dato-seri-najib-razak-quit.

Koike, Yuriko. 2015. "The Trials of Asian Democracy." *Project Syndicate*, March 31.

Koike, Yuriko. 2016. "ASEAN's Destructive Elites." *The Strategist*, March 30. Accessed April 7, 2016. http://www.aspistrategist.org.au/aseans-destructive-elites/).

Lat. 2002. Keynote Speech on "Sketching Asia's Yesterday and Today," 13th Fukuoka Asian Culture Prizes 2002 Public Forum, Fukuoka City, Japan.

Lim, Hong Hai. 2002. "Public Administration: The Effects of Executive Dominance." In *Democracy in Malaysia; Discourses and Practices*, edited by Francis Loh Kok Wah and Khoo Boo Teik. Richmond, United Kingdom: Curzon, 165–197.

Lim, Hong Hai. 2007. "Improving Administrative Performance in Malaysia: The More Difficult Next Steps in Reform." *Policy and Society* 26 (2): 33–59.

Lim, Kit Siang. 1978. *Time Bombs in Malaysia*. Petaling Jaya: Democratic Action Party.

Lopez, Greg. 2015. "Anticorruption Reform in a Setting of Widespread Corruption—The Case of Malaysia." *Forbes*, September 2.

Lopez, Leslie. 2004. "Abdullah Gains in Corruption Fight." *Far Eastern Economic Review*, March 4.

Lourdesamy, I. 2015. "How Good Is Our Government?" *Malaysiakini*, August 4. Accessed April 12, 2016. https://www.malaysiakini.com/letters/307683.

Malaysian Anti-Corruption Commission (MACC). 2015. "Malaysia's Experience, Sharing Good Practices." *MACC Today* (Special Edition) 1: 1–8.

Mahamood, Muliyadi. 2014. "Cartoonist Lat and Malaysian National Identity: An Appreciation." In *Southeast Asian Cartoon Art: History, Trends and Problems*, edited by John A. Lent. Jefferson, NC: McFarland & Company, 205–214.

Malay Mail Online. 2014. "'Corruption' Is First Word on Malaysians' Minds When Thinking of Government, Survey Says." September 25. Accessed April 8, 2016. http://www.themalaymailonline.com/malaysia/article/corruption-is-first-word-on-malaysians-minds-when-thinking-of-government-su.

Malay Mail Online. 2015. "MACC: RM2.6b in Najib's Account from 'Donors,' not 1MDB." August 3. Accessed April 9, 2016. http://www.themalaymailonline.com/malaysia/article/macc-rm2.6b-in-najibs-account-from-donors-not-1mdb.

Malay Mail Online. 2016. "Bersih 2.0 Wins South Korean Human Rights Award." April 22. Accessed April 26, 2016. http://www.themalaymailonline.com/malaysia/article/bersih-2.0-wins-south-korean-human-rights-award.

Malaysia Today. 2010. “Pua Says 1MDB Profits Suspect.” October 9.

Malaysiakini. 2009. “How the Gov’t ‘Looted’ up to US$100 bil.” November 28. Accessed April 18, 2016. https://www.malaysiakini.com/news/118519.

Malaysiakini. 2016a. “Citizens’ Declaration Spells out Demand for Removal of Najib.” March 4. Accessed April 9, 2016. https://www.malaysiakini.com/news/332750.

Malaysiakini. 2016b. “M’kini Poll: 76pct Support Citizens’ Declaration.” March 9.

Mayberry, Kate. 2016. “Malaysia’s Social Media Rebels.” *Aljazeera*, March 15.

Merdeka Center. 2009. “Peninsular Voter Survey 4th Quarter 2008.” Merdeka Center For Opinion Research.

Mokhtar, Mariam. 2015. “A Mahathir-ACA Flashback with Harassment of MACC Officers.” *The Ant Daily*, March 31.

Mokhtar, Mariam. 2016. “What Message Does Khir Toyo’s Release Send to the Public?” *The Ant Daily*, August 12.

Musa, Bakri. 2005. “Federal Minister Isa Samad Out!” June 24. Accessed April 19, 2016. http://www.bakrimusa.com/archives/federal-minister-isa-samad-out.

Musa, M. Bakri. 2001. “Fixing Umno’s Rot.” *Malaysiakini*, February 24. Accessed April 19, 2016. https://www.malaysiakini.com/columns/6701.

Naidu, Sumisha. 2016. “Malaysian Lawyers Call for Attorney-General’s Resignation.” *Channel News Asia*, March 19.

New Straits Times. 2008. “Internet Served a Painful Lesson.” March 26.

New Tactics. 2010. “Empowering Citizens to Fight Corruption.” Accessed April 11, 2016. https://www.newtactics.org/

empowering-citizens-fight-corruption/empowering-citizens-fight-corruption.

O'Grady, Siobhan. 2015. "The Worst Corruption Scandals of 2015." *Foreign Policy*, December 29. Accessed April 8, 2016. http://foreignpolicy.com/2015/12/29/the-worst-corruption-scandals-of-2015/.

Ofosu-Amaah, W. Paatii, Raj Soopramanien, and Kishor Uprety. 1999. *Combating Corruption: A Comparative Review of Selected Legal Aspects of State Practice and Major International Initiatives*. Washington, DC: The World Bank.

Palani, Tarani. 2012. "Punched, Slapped, Kicked." *Free Malaysia Today*, April 29. Accessed April 14, 2016. http://www.freemalaysiatoday.com/category/nation/2012/04/29/punched-slapped-kicked/.

Parameswaran, Prashanth. 2016. "Malaysia a 'New Dictatorship' under Najib: Ex-Deputy Prime Minister." *The Diplomat*, February 28.

Pemandu. 2014. *Government Transformation Programme (GTP) Annual Report*. Putrajaya: Prime Minister's Department.

Ram, Sadho. 2015. "The Gag on The Edge: Who Is Saying What, and How the Paper Is Fighting Back." *SAYS.com*, July 25. Accessed April 12, 2016. http://says.com/my/news/kementrian-dalam-negeri-suspends-the-edge-over-1mdb-reporting.

Roberts, Sir Adam, and Timothy Garton Ash, eds. 2009. *Civil Resistance and Power Politics: The Experience of Non-violent Action from Gandhi to the Present*. Oxford: Oxford University Press.

Saleh, Zakiah, and Haslida Abu Hasan. 2015. "The Role of the Public Accounts Committee in Enhancing Government Accountability in Malaysia." In *Making Governments Accountable: The Role of Public Accounts Committees and National Audit Offices*, edited by Zahirul Hoque. London: Routledge, 209–228.

Schwab, Klaus, ed. 2015. *The Global Competitiveness Report 2015–2016*. Geneva: World Economic Forum.

Singapore Monitor. 1984. "Mahathir Lashes Out at Govt Critics at General Assembly." May 25. Accessed April 19, 2016. http://eresources.nlb.gov.sg/newspapers/Digitised/Article/singmonitor19840525-2.2.13.14.aspx.

Soh, Felix. 2004. "Abdullah Shows He's Serious about War on Corruption." *The Straits Times*, February 11.

Soon, Chuan Yean. 2010. "Zunar, the Multifaceted Cartoonist." *Aliran*, September 25.

Sreenevasan, Ambiga. 2013. "Will Elections in Malaysia be Free or Fair?" *Aljazeera*, May 4.

SUARAM. 2015. *Human Rights Report 2015 Overview: Civil and Political Rights*. Petaling Jaya: Suara Inisiatif Sdn Bhd.

SUHAKAM. 2013. *SUHAKAM Annual Report 2012.* Kuala Lumpur: Human Rights Commission of Malaysia.

SUHAKAM. 2015. *SUHAKAM Annual Report 2014.* Kuala Lumpur: Human Rights Commission of Malaysia.

Tam, Weng Wah. 2010. "PCB Performs Similar Function as Ombudsman." *Malaysiakini*, March 22. Accessed April 16, 2016. https://www.malaysiakini.com/letters/127210.

Tavanti, Marco, and Agata Stachowicz-Stanusch, eds. 2013. "Anti-Corruption for Human Security." *The International Journal of Sustainable Human Security* 1 (1): 1–177.

Teh, Benny Cheng Guan, ed. 2012. *Human Security: Securing East Asia's Future*. Dordrecht: Springer.

Teoh, Shannon. 2016. "Malaysia's Attorney-General Clears Najib of Corruption over Cash Gifts from Saudi Royals." *The Straits*

Times, January 27.

The Economist. 2015. "Malaysia's Masses Protest against Corruption." August 30.

The Guardian. 2016. "Independent Malaysian News Site Closes Amid Government Clampdown on Media." March 15.

The Star. 2014. "NFC—A Four-Year Scandal Comes to a Head." November 6.

The Sun Daily. 2014. "Court Orders Lift of Ban on Cartoonist Zunar's Two Books." October 9.

Theophilus, Claudia. 2008. "Malaysia Poll Battle Goes Online." *Aljazeera*, March 9.

Transparency International–Malaysia. 2014. "Give MACC Prosecution Power." *Malaysiakini*, February 5. Accessed April 14, 2016. https://www.malaysiakini.com/letters/253579.

Ugaz, Jose. 2015. "Who Paid the Money and Why?" Speech Presented at the 16th International Anti-Corruption Conference, Putrajaya, Malaysia, September 2. Accessed April 9, 2016. http://www.transparency.org/news/speech/who_paid_the_money_and_why.

Wolfowitz, Paul. 2006. "Good Governance and Development—A Time for Action." Speech at a conference, Jakarta, Indonesia, April 11. Accessed April 18, 2016. http://go.worldbank.org/BEUNCNX0D0.

Woon, Leven. 2013. "High Tolerance for Graft among Chinese." *Free Malaysia Today*, December 28. Accessed April 8, 2016. http://www.freemalaysiatoday.com/category/nation/2013/12/28/high-tolerance-for-graft-among-chinese/.

Yoon, Szu-Mae. 2003. "TI: Nation Found Wanting in Tackling Corruption." *Malaysiakini*, September 18. Accessed April 14, 2016. https://www.malaysiakini.com/news/17115.

3

Social Construction of Good Governance in Vietnam: Looking for the Meanings of and Implications for Its Development

Tran Van Kham
VNU-University of Social Sciences and Humanities, Vietnam

Introduction

Governance indicators have been published worldwide in many research reports and policy briefs by the United Nations Development Programme (UNDP), Transparency International, and Oxford Poverty and Human Develop Initiative show that Asian countries lag behind other developed countries and present a number of issues related to social development, human development, corruption, the effectiveness of government, voice and accountability, rule of law, and level of poverty.

Despite difficulties in aspects of its society, economic, politics, and culture, Vietnam's social and health indicators suggest its populace is getting wealthier and healthier in comparison to that of other regional countries. In order to sustain its political and social status and growth, Vietnam's government is trying its best to introduce national strategies to maintain better governance, especially in terms of public administration reform (for the period 2010–2015 and 2016–2020). The state also issued a wide range of policies and initiatives to promote the role of public administration and to reduce corruption as well as to enhance citizen participation and the rule of law in daily life. However, the term *good governance* is still limited in current scholarship and social research works in Vietnam; there are more works related to public administration, anticorruption, or local participation. Pioneering research in Vietnam on the rule of law, which is related to good governance ideas, is currently being implemented by the Center for Community Support Development Studies (CECODES), Vietnam Father Land Front, and the UNDP in Vietnam as the PAPI's annual surveys. The PAPI presents comprehensive ideas to understand public administration at the provincial level in Vietnam and currently is known to offer significant implication for governance in this country.

This research aims to answer the following research questions: (a) How are these indexes constructed in Vietnamese contexts? (b) How is the good governance socially constructed from the voice of citizens? (c) What are the implications found in these indexes and voices to improve governance and administrations in Vietnam? and (d) What are suggestions for further research on good governance in the social research in Vietnam?

In order to find the evidence and explanations for such research questions, this research applies the theoretical perspective of social constructionism. In this approach, which is based on the studies of Berger and Luckmann (1966), all knowledge is socially constructed, including the knowledge of what is real. The term *social constructionism* refers to a tradition of scholars tracing the origin of knowledge and meaning as well as the nature of reality to processes generated with human relationships (Given 2008, 816). Social constructionism has been applied widely in social research, making significant contributions to the study of deviances, social problems, social movements, the self, gender, race, education, health, emotions, the family, and other areas (Holstein & Miller 1993; Hosking 1999; Harris 2010; Lock & Strong 2010). To distinguish between the use of social constructionism and constructivism, Franklin (1995) outlines six differences and similarities. The perspectives are similar in that (a) they emphasize human agency and assert that reality is socially and/or psychologically constructed; (b) they do not believe in an objective reality; (c) they both see the importance of language and social processes as affecting the ability to know an objective reality comprehensively. The concepts differ as follows: (a) the importance of cognitive structures and developmental processes for constructivists versus language, culture, and the social process in forming constructions and understandings for social constructionists; (b) constructivists are more experimental/ clinical in their approaches; and (c) social constructionists focus on social-contextual issues and people' stories (Franklin 1995, 396-397; Rogers & Pilgrim 2005, 15). On the basis of the main ideas of social constructionism, Kham (2013) mentioned that its application is compatible with the Vietnamese context as follows:

- Concerning the research process, social constructionism is a guideline for selecting a suitable methodology and methods as well as theoretical stances for research topics relating to meaning generation or the experiences of research participants.
- Using the social constructionist approach, social problems as the content of social research are viewed as being generated in social context, as products of social claiming, labelling, and other constitutive processes. This application supports researchers to use the approach for identifying, analyzing, and making recommendations relating to social problems as research problems
- With those research topics relating to vulnerable groups or sensitive groups, social researchers are able to apply this approach to drive suitable methodology and methods for collecting data as well as generating the meaning of research problems. Research relating to "constructing of X (a research problem)" is acknowledged with unending lists in social research, which is a evidence of the prospect and ability of social constructionism in reality of research.
- As an epistemological background, social constructionism drives researchers to identify a suitable theoretical framework, methodology, research methods, and methods for analyzing data. Such driving creates a research process with four elements as stated by Crotty (1998). This

> process is clear and applicable when collecting data in the context of Vietnam and with Vietnamese respondents. In particular, it is easy to apply to those research topics on sensitive problems and need a long time for approaching the respondents and understanding their daily life experiences. Social constructionism is very useful in social research on Vietnamese culture, people with disabilities, marginalized people, vulnerable groups, and minority groups as well as with marginalized people, the poor, and people in crisis.
> (Kham 2013, 35–36)

On the basis on this theoretical perspective, good governance will be socially constructed in Vietnam by the voice of local people, and it drives this chapter's research methodology and methods in terms of document analysis, observations, and surveys. This chapter uses the raw data taken by CECODES and UNDP in Vietnam in the annual survey of the provincial administration index. In addition, on comparing the data from The World Bank, Toward Transparency, and Transparency International, the research method of document analysis is used to provide the basic information for further understanding of good governance in Vietnam.

General Understanding of Governance

The idea of governance has wide meanings, particularly in terms of its implications for driving the society and economy to meet social needs (Pierre 2000). The concept is quite common in political science, public administration, and development management. It goes with terms such as *democracy*, *civil society*, *citizen participation*, *human rights*, and *sustainable development* (Agera 2000)· In the last few years, this concept fell deeply into the public sector reform and was regarded as an aspect of the new paradigm in public administration with a focus on the role of public managers and administrators in providing good public services; advocating managerial autonomy; reducing central agency controls; supplying the demands, measures, and rewards for both organizational and individual performance; recognizing the importance of providing human and technological resources; being receptive to competition and open-minded about public performance by public servants (Commonwealth Association of Public Administration and Management 1995). The term *governance* is trending now, but it has a long history. The word traces back to the Greek, meaning to pilot and steer or how to develop rules and make decisions. By the end of 1960s, this term had a prominent role in constructing the debates and discourse in the social sciences. Since the 1990s, this word has become a buzzword, a hot topic in the social sciences. It has evolved with different meanings from different approaches and contexts. There is not a consensus on the unique meanings, nature, and form of governance. Moreover, there is a debate about the relation between governing and governance. The former covers ideas of steering, controlling, or managing society, whereas the latter refers to the forms developed from governing activities (interaction among multiple actors) (Jamil 2016). The term *governance* encompasses the influence of multiple authorities including nongovernment actors such as civil society, donor organizations, and individual participants.

The World Bank coined the term of *good governance* in 1989, which attracted the attention and participation of many international agencies to identify the essential components and factors. Then, the Worldwide Governance Indicators (WGI) or the Corruption Perception Index (CPI) was introduced and applied widely. Data taken from these indexes help the scholars and readers to understand the status of each country from a governance perspective. Overall, governance has the following structure:

- the relationship between governments and the markets;
- the relationship between governments and citizens;
- the relationship between governments and the voluntary or private sector;
- the relationship between elected (politicians) and appointed (civil servants);
- the relationship between local government institutions and urban/rural dwellers;
- the relationship between legislature and the executive; and
- the relationship between national states and international institutions.

In political science, *governance* refers to the activity

and process of public authority for the realization of the public interest. Governance and government have similarities, but there are significant differences. The first difference is that the main part of government consists of authority units, but the main structure of governance could be either governmental or nongovernmental organizations, or even a combination of the governmental and private sectors. The focus of government is the government itself, whereas governance focuses on society as a whole. Just as government can be good or bad, governance could also be good or bad as well.

Good Governance: Concepts, Principles, and Measures

Good governance is a management process that maximizes the public interest, and it has been an attractive topic in social sciences recently. The essential characteristics of good governance are the cooperative management of public life by both government and citizens; a new relationship between political state and civil society; and the best political situation involving public and private actors and governmental and civil organizations (Agnafors 2000; Zhenglai and Guo, 2011, 16–17). From such ideas, good governance combines its components as rule of law, participation, fairness, transparency, accountability, efficiency, stability, and integrity (Zhenglai and Guo,

2011). These components can be analyzed as follows:

1. The rule of law—that is, the belief that the law is the highest authority in public and political management, everyone is equal before the law, and enforcement of laws should be impartial.
2. Participation, which refers to political participation by citizens in social and political life, and not only political participation but also civic participation in other areas of social life.
3. Fairness, which refers to equality with regard to political rights and economic rights for citizens of different genders, classes, races, educational qualifications, and religious and political beliefs.
4. Transparency—that is, information is accessible to all citizens.
5. Accountability, which mainly means that governmental and nongovernmental organizations are accountable to the public or to those whose interests may be affected by their decisions.
6. Efficiency, which mainly refers to management efficiency that makes the best use of resources for public interests.
7. Stability, which refers to peace, order, safety, solidarity, cohesive public policy, and so on.
8. Integrity, which means that government officials and other institutional decision makers obey the law, are clean and honest, do not abuse their power for personal gains, or seek

rent through their own power.

(Yu 1999)

The term *good governance* has been reviewed and criticized by Farazmand (2004) because this concept does not cover the global power structure, and the bad or the good is unilaterally identified by the global power elites to seek global capitalism. Farazman also proposed the concept of *sound governance* to include the global element of governance, which is open for indigenous solutions. Grindle (2007) posited that the good governance agenda may become comprehensive and complex. She introduced the concept of *good enough governance* to imply that "all good things cannot be purchased at once." Jamil (2016) presents the understandings of good governance in the following terms:

(a) *governance* denotes exercise of authority and power;

(b) governance involves interdependence among a host of actors for the sake of policy making at multiple levels (i.e., not only government organizations but also others such as nongovernment actors and private business companies);

(c) these diverse relationships to be governed at multiple levels required rule making, rule following, and rule enforcement;

(d) the meaning of governance is broader than government and emphasizes the role of network beyond the hierarchy and markets modes of governing. The network operates at national, international, and transnational levels.

(Jamil 2016, 14-15)

In approaching the negative side of governance (poor

governance), the main implications are as follows:

- failure to make a clear distinction between what is public and private, hence a tendency to divert public resources for private gain;
- failure to establish a predictable framework of law, government behavior and the rule of law;
- excessive rules and regulations that impede the functioning of markets;
- priorities inconsistent with development, resulting in a misallocation of resources;
- excessively narrow or nontransparent decision-making processes;
- lack of a code of conduct in managing the affairs of the state;
- lack of clearly defined policy assumptions.

(Agera 2000, 4)

So, the absence of good governance or the appearance of bad governance damages the role of government, and leads to poverty and less sustainable development of a society. Many consider good governance as the means and ends for the public administration and social development. It is conceptualized as a part of the development process, an instrument of the state, a facilitator in the development process, a significant way to deliver good services to the public. Recent research presents the key elements of good governance in terms of accountability, transparency, combating corruption, stakeholder participation, and a legal and judical framework (Agera

2000, 8-10).

In addition, in 2004 the Institute on Governance in Ottawa, Canada, proposed five main principles for good governance in the twenty-first century in combination with the UNDP principles for human development: legitimacy and voice (participation and consensus orientation), direction (strategic action), performance (responsive and effectiveness and efficiency), accountability (accountability and transparency), and fairness (equity and rule of law) (Graham et al. 2003). Similarly, the Council of Europe presented its twelve principles for good local governance, as seen in Table 1.

Table 1. Twelve principles for good local governance by Conduct of Elections

Principle 1 - Fair CoE, representation and participation	• Local elections are conducted freely and fairly, according to international standards and national legislation, and without any fraud. • Citizens are at the center of public activity and they are involved in clearly defined ways in public life at local level. • All men and women can have a voice in decision making, either directly or through legitimate intermediate bodies that represent their interests. Such broad participation is built on the freedoms of expression, assembly and association. • All voices, including those of the less privileged and most vulnerable, are heard and taken into account in decision making, including over the allocation of resources. • There is always an honest attempt to mediate between various legitimate interests and to reach a broad consensus on what is in the best interest of the whole community and on how this can be achieved. • Decisions are taken according to the will of the many, while the rights and legitimate interests of the few are respected.

Principle 2 – Responsiveness	• Objectives, rules, structures, and procedures are adapted to the legitimate expectations and needs of citizens. • Public services are delivered, and requests and complaints are responded to within a reasonable timeframe.
Principle 3 - Efficiency and Effectiveness	• Results meet the agreed objectives. • Best possible use is made of the resources available. • Performance management systems make it possible to evaluate and enhance the efficiency and effectiveness of services. • Audits are carried out at regular intervals to assess and improve performance.
Principle 4 - Openness and Transparency	• Decisions are taken and enforced in accordance with rules and regulations. • There is public access to all information that is not classified for well-specified reasons as provided for by law (such as the protection of privacy or ensuring the fairness of procurement procedures). • Information on decisions, implementation of policies and results is made available to the public in such a way as to enable it to effectively follow and contribute to the work of the local authority.
Principle 5 - Rule of Law	• The local authorities abide by the law and judicial decisions. • Rules and regulations are adopted in accordance with procedures provided for by law and are enforced impartially.
Principle 6 - Ethical Conduct	• The public good is placed before individual interests. • There are effective measures to prevent and combat all forms of corruption. • Conflicts of interest are declared in a timely manner and persons involved must abstain from taking part in relevant decisions.
Principle 7 - Competence and Capacity	• The professional skills of those who deliver governance are continuously maintained and strengthened in order to improve their output and impact. • Public officials are motivated to continuously improve their performance. • Practical methods and procedures are created and used in order to transform skills into capacity and to produce better results.

Principle 8 - Innovation and Openness to Change	• New and efficient solutions to problems are sought and advantage is taken of modern methods of service provision. • There is readiness to pilot and experiment new programs and to learn from the experience of others. • A climate favorable to change is created in the interest of achieving better results.
Principle 9 - Sustainability and Long-term Orientation	• The needs of future generations are taken into account in current policies. • The sustainability of the community is constantly taken into account. • Decisions strive to internalize all costs and not to transfer problems and tensions, be they environmental, structural, financial, economic or social, to future generations. • There is a broad and long-term perspective on the future of the local community along with a sense of what is needed for such development. • There is an understanding of the historical, cultural, and social complexities in which this perspective is grounded.
Principle 10 - Sound Financial Management	• Charges do not exceed the cost of services provided and do not reduce demand excessively, particularly in the case of important public services. • Prudence is observed in financial management, including in the contracting and use of loans, in the estimation of resources, revenues and reserves, and in the use of exceptional revenue. • Multi-annual budget plans are prepared, with consultation of the public. • Risks are properly estimated and managed, including by the publication of consolidated accounts and, in the case of public-private partnerships, by sharing the risks realistically. • The local authority takes part in arrangements for inter-municipal solidarity, fair sharing of burdens and benefits and reduction of risks (e.g., equalization systems, intermunicipal cooperation, mutualization of risks).

Principle 11 - Human Rights, Cultural Diversity and Social Cohesion	• Within the local authority's sphere of influence, human rights are respected, protected and implemented, and discrimination on any grounds is combated. • Cultural diversity is treated as an asset, and continuous efforts are made to ensure that all have a stake in the local community, identify with it and do not feel excluded. • Social cohesion and the integration of disadvantaged areas are promoted. • Access to essential services is preserved, in particular for the most disadvantaged sections of the population.
Principle 12 – Accountability	• All decision makers, collective and individual, take responsibility for their decisions. • Decisions are reported on, explained, and can be sanctioned. • There are effective remedies against maladministration and against actions of local authorities which infringe civil rights.

Source: http://www.coe.int/t/dgap/localdemocracy/Strategy_Innovation/12principles_en.asp

Social Construction of Good Governance in Vietnam

Vietnam in Development: Implications from Different Indicators

Since 1986, as a milestone of the Renewal Policy (*Đổi Mới*), Vietnam achieved significant outcomes in many aspects of life. The critical one is the improvement in the Human Development Index (HDI).

Table 2. **The Human Development Index: Vietnam among the region's countries**

	2000	2010	2011	2012	2013	2014
Vietnam	0.575	0.653	0.657	0.660	0.638	0.666
Indonesia	0.606	0.665	0.671	0.678	0.684	0.684
Thailand	0.648	0.716	0.721	0.723	0.722	0.726
China	0.588	0.699	0.707	0.718	0.719	0.727
Malaysia	0.723	0.769	0.772	0.774	0.733	0.779
Japan	0.857	0.884	0.886	0.888	0.890	0.891
Korea, South	0.821	0.886	0.891	0.893	0.895	0.898

Source: http://hdr.undp.org/en/composite/trends

Vietnam's HDI has significantly improved since 1990, with a small drop in 2013; however, its statistics still stands behind other countries in the region. It shows the great efforts by the government on making life conditions better for all.

Among the indicators of HDI, a prominent change is presented in the gross national income (GNI) in USD per capita in 2014, which is more than four times that of the year 1980 and twice that of the year 2000.

Table 3. **Vietnam's HDI trends based on consistent time-series data and new goalposts**

	Life expectancy at birth	Expected years of schooling	Mean years of schooling	GNI per capita (USD)	HDI value
1980	67.6	8.6	4.2	1,080	0.463
1985	69.0	8.1	4.3	1,349	0,479
1990	70.5	7.7	3.9	1,410	0,475
1995	72.0	9.2	4.6	2,020	0.530
2000	73.3	10.4	5.4	2,615	0.575
2005	74.3	11.2	6.4	3,423	0.616
2010	75.1	11.9	7.5	4,314	0.653
2011	75.3	11.9	7.5	4,514	0.657

2012	75.5	11.9	7.5	4,709	0.660
2013	75.6	11.9	7.5	4,906	0.663
2014	75.8	11.9	7.5	5,092	0.666

Source: http://hdr.undp.org/en/composite/HDI

Table 2 shows Vietnam's overall HDI; Table 3 presents the specific indicators of HDI in terms of life expectancy at birth, expected years of schooling, mean year of schooling, GNI per capita, and HDI value. The overall trend of these indicators has consistently increased since 1980. The HDI value has its significant increased ratio since 2010. Furthermore, Vietnam is ranked 126th among the 188 countries, with in the group of medium human development.

Table 4. Vietnam's HDI Indicators for 2014 Relative to Selected Countries and Groups

	HDI value	HDI rank	Life expectancy at birth	Expected years of schooling	Mean years of schooling	GNI per capita (PPP USD)
Vietnam	0.666	116	75.8	11.9	7.5	5,092
Thailand	0.726	93	74.4	13.5	7.3	13,323
Philippines	0.668	115	68.2	11.3	8.9	7,915
East Asia and the Pacific	0.710	—	74.0	12.7	7.5	11,449
Medium HDI	0.630	—	68.6	11.8	6.2	6,353

Source: http://hdr.undp.org/en/composite/HDI

Vietnam's HDI is lower than the average among countries in East Asia and the Pacific but slightly higher than the medium HDI in the world. This shows that Vietnam has been achieving a significant development index in the last few decades, but its HDI rank still belongs to the low medium group and lags far behind countries in the region.

The achievement of HDI also presents the view of a well-organized state in keeping the whole society on its development and stability. This achievement also implies the role of the government in steering the whole society to overcome difficulties immediately after wartime and in the globalization process.

Ho Chi Minh's Ideas about (Good) Government: Specific Perspective for Constructing Good Governance in Vietnam

The form of the Vietnamese government

The government has been constructed in Vietnam following the ideas of "belonging to the people, by the people and for the people" as suggested by President Ho Chi Minh, presented all ideas about the meaning of "*all powers belonging to the people*" (Vietnam National Assembly 1946: article 1), people are the subjects of state powers that originate from the people's power. The first article of the State Constitution in 1946 stated that "*Vietnam is a country of the democratic republic. All authorities in the countries belong to the Vietnamese people irrespective of race, sex, wealth, class, religion"*. In addition, Article 32 of the Constitution states that "*those activities related to the national destiny will be made by the people"*(Vietnam National Assembly 1946). It is a form of referendum and democratic mode that was constructed early in Vietnam. The people's democratic nature is the prominent feature of the new type of state government. In Vietnam, the people held all the power; the state agencies organized by the people and state employees who authorized and carried out the people's aspiration became the servants of the people. The democratic republic has fundamentally changed the political power relations and the exercise of power in that the people are placed in the highest position and the state is no longer the dominant tool, as in the enslaved, feudalist, and capitalist states.

From such ideas by Ho Chi Minh, in this form of the State, the people implemented their ownership with the fundamental right to vote to form the national government and local administrative governments. Government is an organization elected by the people to exercise the rights of the people. The national election policy proposed in 1946 by Ho Chi Minh represented his will. "General election is an opportunity for the whole national freedom to choose talented people, to take on the work ethics of the country... General Election is freedom, equality, i.e., democracy and solidarity" (Hồ Chí Minh 2000a, 133). Regarding the way to form the government, his idea is presented thus: "In the general election, everyone who wants to take care of the country, has the right to stand for election; everyone who is a citizen shall have the right to vote ...

By these elections, the Congress is formed. Congress will appoint a government. That government belongs to the whole nation" (Hồ Chí Minh 2000a, 133). Through the elected National Assembly and the Government, the people exercise their power in the forms of direct and representative democracy.

The supreme power of the people is not only reflected in the election of the National Assembly and People's Councils at all levels but also in the power to remove, control, and monitor the activities of the participants. This democratic mechanism constructs the National Assembly cleanly to maintain quality and operational capacity. Ho Chi Minh stated, "The people have the right to dismiss the National Assembly and People's Council deputies if she or he have proved unworthy of the trust of the people" (Hồ Chí Minh 2000c, 591).

The form of "Government of the people and by the people" also implies an important concept: the people have control of the State. Ho Chi Minh wrote, "Our government is government of the people. The only purpose is to serve the interests of the people. The Government hopes to help people, urging critics to control and fulfill their duty as faithful servants of the people's devotion" (Hồ Chí Minh 2000b, 391–392). With State ownership, implementing the people's mandate, elected delegates shall have a close and intimate relationship with people in order to understand them, listen to the opinions of the people with a sense of responsibility and the goal of practical problem solving for the whole country and for the people. From the viewpoint of Ho Chi Minh, in order to represent workers as the State owners, the elected representatives must have regular contacts with the people. If this connection is lacking, the State can very easily fall into bureaucracy and stagnation, opposing the true democratic nature of the new form of the State.

As the State owner, the people have rights through the mechanism of the democratic exercise of power, but at the same time, the people have the obligation to build and defend the State and improve its transparency and strength. Ho Chi Minh always required the people as the owner of the State to have the goals of independence, freedom, so all their rights and duties should be linked to each other. According to Ho Chi Minh's ideology, the State of the people, by the people, and for the people should be democratic and demonstrate the power of the workers as well as enforcement of the workers' power. This perspective is known as the overall direction and thread for whole process of building the new kind of Vietnamese State. The Vietnamese Constitution in 1946 and its amendments in 1959, 1980, 1992, and 2013 have always shown such an implication. In the Renewal process, making this form of Government is a key aspect of strengthening and renewing the organization and operations of the State.

Unique mission of the government: To serve the people's interests

The Vietnamese government is democratic in fact and action. Shortly after the August revolution in 1945, Ho Chi Minh highlighted the fundamental differences in quality between the Democratic Republic of Vietnam and its earlier forms: "we must understand that staffs in the government agencies, from central to locals, are servants of the people, i.e., are those who should do all for the people, not to crush the people as under colonialism by Japan and France. We must do our best for whatever benefits the people; we must refrain from whatever is harmful to them" (Hồ Chí Minh 2000a, 56-57). Ho Chi Minh always advised officials to pay attention to those recommendations and proposals by the people: "It should be noted to solve all issues, especially those related to people's lives, although they seem difficult. They should accept the appealing application by the people and do the fairness for them. They should carefully take care of the relief work for victims, paying attention to anti-illiteracy among the people. In short, everything that can improve the material and spiritual life of our people must receive special attention" (Hồ Chí Minh 2000a, 47–48).

On the relationship between the State and the people, Ho Chi Minh stated: "without the people, the government has not enough force. Without the government, there is no leading force for the people to follow. So, the government and the people must unite as a team" (Hồ Chí Minh 2000a, 56). The basic internal functions of Government are to guide people to have better lives, a high rate of production, saving money practice, and to gradually improve the material and spiritual life in order to satisfy their daily needs. Ho Chi Minh also suggested that "We compete to be free and independent; however, in such a free and independent life, people still die by starvation, by cold, so freedom and independence are worth little. People only know the value of freedom and independence when they are safe with enough food and clothing. We must immediately

(a) make sure people have enough food to eat, (b) make sure people have enough clothes to wear, (c) make sure people have a place to live, (d) make sure people have educational opportunities. Our government aims go to such things, so our people deserve to live in a free and independent country and they can contribute to the liberty and independence of the country"(Hồ Chí Minh 2000a,152).

From the perspective of Ho Chi Minh, the indicator of good government is that all these needs are satisfied. To do that, it is necessary to have a clean governing mechanism. If the operation of the state is inefficient and bureaucratic, the civil service staff (especially the senior ones) are degraded; such a State has slipped away from the democratic trajectory and becomes a force in opposition to the people's interest and will. Through his political sensitivities and practical experiences, Ho Chi Minh early detected and warned of the social disease of distorting and corrupting the State. In his opinion, social administration and management is a difficult task, but it will improve when the State prioritizes the people's interests and the civil staff learn diligently and work hard to improve their skills for better completion of tasks.

Current Ideas about Good Governance in Vietnam

There are not various views in Vietnam about good governance, there is only some perspective presenting the consideration to public administration currently. It is clearly identified in national initiatives and actions for improving the efficiency of public administration and local administrative units. Among the efforts by the Vietnamese government to improve public administration, the most significant initiative is the PAPI (the Vietnamese provincial governance and public administration performance index) supported by the UNDP and implemented systematically since 2009. This index provides a measure of the State's efficiency in improving the public administration in Vietnam during last few years. The PAPI covers six dimensions and twenty-two sub-dimensions, including ninety-two indicators developed from different perspectives on governance and good governance worldwide. The PAPI aims to look at the overall trend of government performance in Vietnam at the provincial level. This index is a policy monitoring tool that reflects citizen experiences with central to local governments in performing governance, public administration, and public service delivery functions. It helps to create motivation for public officials, civil servants, and public employees at different levels and in different sectors to perform better in public sector management and public service delivery. The index ultimately aims at better servicing citizens and fostering national development. The PAPI has been applied in Vietnam since 2009 as the annual indicator for public administration. It was conducted in only nine provinces at first, but now it covers all provinces in Vietnam.

Table 5. **A snapshot of PAPI**

What PAPI measures:
Content: Six dimensions, 22 subdimensions, 92 indicators
Method: Face-to-face interviews with a questionnaire comprising 516 items
Who:
- 2009: 543 (3 provinces, 40.33% women and 59.67% men)
- 2010: 5,568 (30 provinces, 47.56% women and 52.44% men)
- 2011: 13,642 (52.96% women and 47.04% men)
- 2012: 13,747 (52.66% women and 47.34% en)
- 2013: 13,892 (52.68% women and 47.32% men)
- 2014: 13,522 (52.94% women and 47.06% men)
- 2015: 13,955 (54,12% women and 45.88% men)
Where: Across 63 provinces and municipalities in Vietnam since 2011 (207 districts, 414 communes, 828 villages)

Source: Recalculated from PAPI reports from 2011 to 2015.

Good Governance in Vietnam: Perspective from Different Indicators

This section covers six aspects constructing the governance/good governance in Vietnam from the main findings taken in the PAPI, CPI, and WGI recently presented.

Good Governance from the WGI

The WGI project reports aggregate and individual governance indicators for 215 economies over the period 1996–2014, for six dimensions of governance: W1. voice and accountability;

W2. political stability and absence of violence; W3. government effectiveness; W4. regulatory quality; W5. rule of law; and W6. control of corruption. These aggregate indicators combine the views of a large number of enterprise, citizen, and expert survey respondents in industrial and developing countries. They are based on more than 30 individual data sources produced by a variety of survey institutes, think tanks, nongovernmental organizations, international organizations, and private sector firms.

Vietnam's statistics based on the WGI are presented in Figure 1.

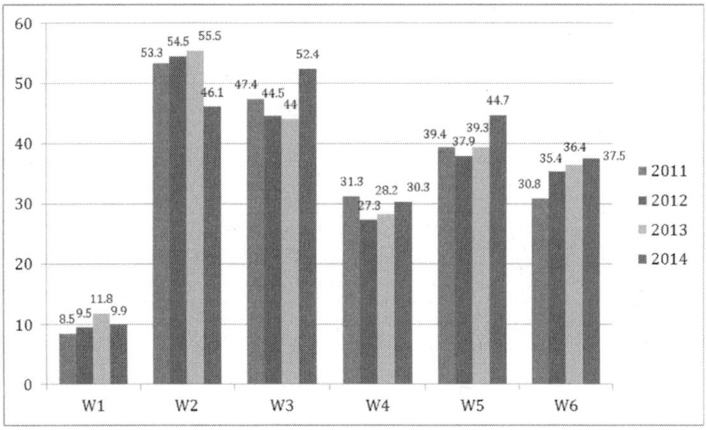

Figure 1. Overview of Vietnam's WGI from 2011 to 2014 (Worldbank, 2016).

The figure shows that W1 has the lowest scores, whereas W2 and W3 have the highest, presenting the implication that voice and accountability in public administration and governance in Vietnam is quite weak. There is a big drop in W2 and a big increase in W3 in 2014 (around 9 percent). As seen in the graph, scores for W4 and W5 show the same trend over the whole period. Assessment of the government effectiveness of Vietnam significantly increased in 2014 (an 8 percent rise, compared with 2013). Only W6 (control of corruption) constantly increased over the period of 2011 to 2014. This shows the international acknowledgement of the Vietnamese government's initiatives and efforts on anti-corruption.

Good Governance from the Voice of CPI

The CPI measures the perceived levels of public sector corruption worldwide. The index draws on different assessments and business opinion surveys carried out by independent and reputable institutions. The surveys and assessments used to compile the index include questions relating to the bribery of public officials, kickbacks in public procurement, embezzlement of public funds, and questions that probe the strength and effectiveness of public-sector anti-corruption efforts.

On the basis of information taken by Transparency International, Figure 2 shows Vietnam's CPI compared with those of other countries in the region.

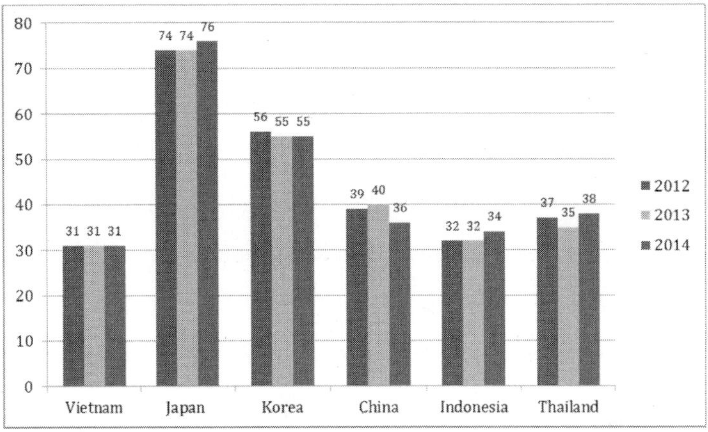

Figure 2. Vietnam's CPI in comparison to the other countries in the region.

Source: Recalculated from reports at http://transparency.org

Good Governance from the Voice of PCI

What is PCI? Introduced in 2005, the Provincial Competitiveness Index (PCI) on Vietnam's business environment conducts an annual business survey, assessment and ranking of the economic governance quality of provincial authorities in creating a favorable business environment for development of the private sector.

What does the PCI measure? The overall PCI comprises ten subindices, reflecting economic governance areas that affect private sector development. A province that is considered to perform well on the PCI is the one that has 1) low entry costs for business start-up; 2) easy access to land and security of the business premises; 3) a transparent business environment and equitable business information; 4) minimal informal charges; 5) limited time requirements for bureaucratic procedures and inspections; 6) limited crowding out of private activity from policy biases toward state, foreign, or connected firms; 7) proactive and creative provincial leadership in solving problems for enterprises; 8) developed and high-quality business support services; 9) sound labor training policies; and 10) fair and effective legal procedures for dispute resolution.

The PCI is constructed in a three-step sequence, referred to as "the 3 Cs": 1) collect business survey data and published data sources, 2) calculate nine subindices and standardize to a 10-point scale, and 3) calibrate the composite PCI as the weighted mean of nine subindices with a maximum score of 100 points.

Table 5. The Overall Trend of PCI in Vietnam since 2011

	Scale (min)	Scale (max)	2011	2012	2013	2014	2015
PCI	1	100	59.43	57.02	56.18	58.07	58.32
Entry costs	1	10	8.54	8.73	7.33	8.30	8.42
Land access	1	10	6.48	6.52	6.63	5.81	5.92
Transparency	1	10	5.84	5.78	5.51	6.05	6.17
Time costs	1	10	6.63	5.72	6.16	6.55	6.65
Informal charges	1	10	6.82	6.47	6.37	5.05	5.13
Bias	1	10	–	–	5.49	5.15	4.93
Proactivity	1	10	4.74	8.85	5.44	4.57	4.68
Business support services	1	10	3.68	3.87	5.12	5.62	5.57
Labor training	1	10	4.77	4.94	5.26	5.80	5.76
Legal institutions	1	10	5.66	3.55	5.45	5.81	5.78

Source: Recalculated from reports at http://transparency.org

It is found that the PCI goes down slightly from 59.43 in 2011 to 56.18 in 2013 and then goes up to 58.32 in 2015. On a scale where 100 is the best PCI, it seems that the governance performance of the provincial government just stands at the average status. Among the ten sub-indicators, because Vietnam has a special policy for investment, the low entry costs for start-ups got better responses, whereas the bias and proactivity show the low responses by the service users.

Changes of Good Governance in Vietnam since 2011 from the PAPI Statistics

Overview of changes

These aspects are developed from the six subdimensions of the PAPI, and experiences of conducting research about the government/governance worldwide, as follows:

D1. Participation at the local levels

D2. Transparency

D3. Vertical accountability

D4. Control of corruption

D5. Public administration procedures

D6. Public service delivery

These six dimensions cover twenty-two subdimensions and ninety-two indicators calculated from structured interviews comprising 516 substantial questions. The scale for these dimensions is from 1 to 10 (lowest to highest administrative performance or governance at provincial level). The changes of governance in Vietnam since 2011 on the basis of such dimensions are significant, as seen in the overview presented in Figure 3:

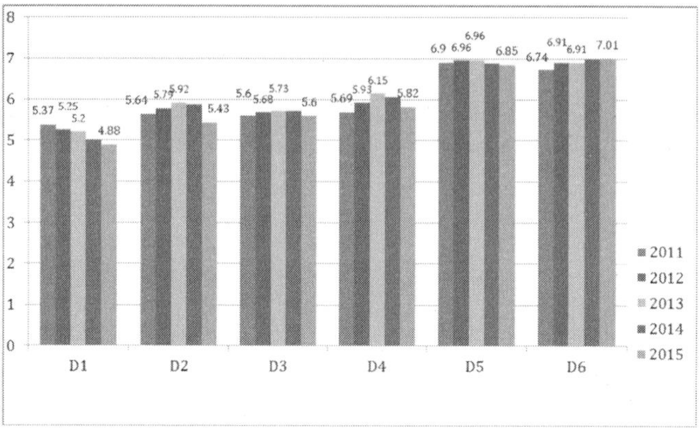

Figure 3: Vietnam's overall PAPI (scale of 1 to 10; higher is better)
Sources: Recalculated from PAPI reports from 2011 to 2015; (CECODES et al. 2016).

It is notable that D1 witnesses a drop through the period, whereas vertical accountability maintains a stable but small increase (from 5.6 to 5.73); D6 moves in the same direction. D2, D4, and D5 see increases in 2012 and 2013, then slightly drop in 2014 and 2015. Overall, D1 receives the lowest score, D5 and D6 get the highest, and D2, D3, and D4 fall in the middle of the scale. However, all six of these dimensions stand at the middle rate of "good governance" in Vietnam's context. It means that the overall governance in Vietnam in terms of public administration decreased through the Government term (2011–2016).

Changes of participation at the local level

This first dimension is regarded in the Constitution as comprising the fundamental rights for all Vietnamese citizens, as the way to implement the Grassroots Democracy Ordinance (*Pháp Lệnh Dân chủ Cơ sở*). Data taken from PAPI shows that most of the highest performing provinces in 2014 are in the northern and central regions of Vietnam, except for Ba RiaVung Tau in the south. This dimension includes four subdimensions with nineteen indicators:

- ***Civic knowledge***: civic knowledge, knows grassroots democracy decree, aware of people know, people decide, correct term limit of 2.5 years
- ***Opportunity for participation***: voted in the commune's last people's council election, voted in the last national assembly election, village head elected, participated in village head election.
- ***Quality of elections:*** more than one candidate, invited to participate, paper ballot was used, votes were counted publicly; candidate was not suggested and voted for winner.
- ***Voluntary contributions***: voluntary contribution to project, community monitoring board, monitors contribution, volunteer contribution recorded, participated in decision making to start project, and provided input to project design.

Table 7. Overall Trend of Local Participation by the Citizens

Subdimensions	Scale (min)	Scale (max)	2011	2012	2013	2014	2015
Civic knowledge	0.25	2.5	1.11	1.06	1.04	1.00	0.96
Opportunities for participation	0.25	2.5	1.88	1.82	1.75	1.66	1.46
Quality of elections	0.25	2.5	1.45	1.47	1.49	1.45	1.44
Voluntary contributions	0.25	2.5	0.85	0.81	0.87	0.81	0.85

Sources: Recalculated from PAPI reports from 2011 to 2015 (CECODES et al. 2016)

In general, it is shown that the degree of local participation by citizens decreased in the period of 2011 to 2015. The same trend happened in the subdimensions 1 and 2, whereas the other two peaked in 2013 before reaching their lowest in 2015. This shows that recent local participation remains far below expectations to improve governance in Vietnam. In addition, the implications from the four subdimensions also presents the individual value prior to the collective and the perception prior to the practices while talking about the participation at the local level by Vietnamese local people. The local people also demonstrate that the practices in the villages are attracted the participation more than those higher level activities.

Transparency of local decision making

The second dimension is transparency of local decision making, with three subdimensions and fifteen indicators.

- ***Poverty Lists***: consists of indicators on poverty list published in last twelve months, type I errors on poverty lists (% disagreed), type II errors on poverty lists (% disagreed).
- ***Commune budgets***: commune budget is made available; respondent has read commune budget and believes accuracy of budget.
- ***Land use planning/price:*** aware of local land plans, comment on local land plan, land plan acknowledge your concerns, impact of land plan on your family, did not lose land as a result of land plan; compensation close to market value; informed of land usage; land use for original purpose; and know where to go to get land price information.

The PAPI measures citizens' "right to know" about the state policies and legal documents that daily affect their livelihood. In perceiving these subdimensions, the transparency is significant.

Table 8. Overall Trend of Transparency in Vietnam's PAPI

Subdimensions	Scale (min)	Scale (max)	2011	2012	2013	2014	2015
Poverty lists	0.33	3.3	2.15	2.23	2.28	2.25	2.06
Commune budgets	0.33	3.3	1.76	1.77	1.85	1.78	1.61
Land use planning/pricing	0.34	3.4	1.56	1.61	1.68	1.72	1.62

Sources: Recalculated from PAPI reports from 2011 to 2015; CECODES et al. 2016)

Local people ranked the poverty lists higher than the commune budget and land use planning/price. The ratio to these subdimensions dropped in 2015.

On looking at the local government's transparency in some aspects of the poverty lists, it was found that the transparency seems to be negative in 2015 compared with previous years, as shown in the graph in Figure 4.

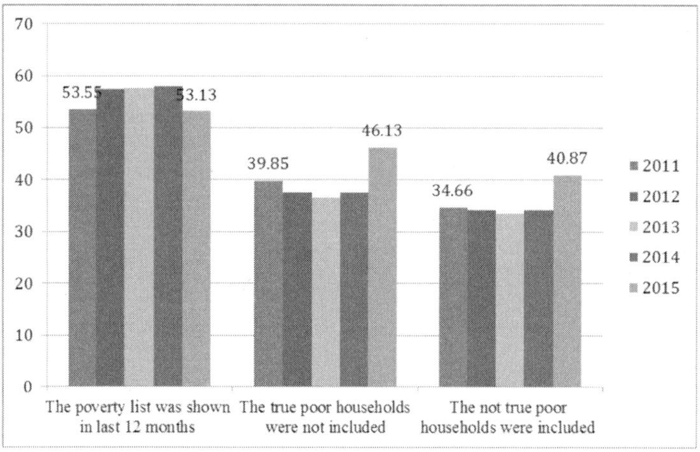

Figure 4: Transparency in Vietnam in the poverty listing (%)

Sources: Recalculated from PAPI reports from 2011 to 2015; CECODES et al. 2016)

PAPI's report in 2015 also shows the reduction of the transparency in most areas related to the issues of commune budgets, the validity of these budgets, the land usage planning, and the actual compensation rate to the land retrieved for the industrial zones and residential purposes. These have recently become urgent, hot topics in Vietnam.

Vertical accountability

The vertical accountability in the PAPI is measured by three subdimensions, with eleven indicators as follows:

- *Interaction with local authorities*: contacts village head; contacts commune government; contact with village head successful; contact with commune successful; made a proposal for authorities; proposal successful;
- *People inspection board*: village has people inspection board; people inspection board set up by vote; people inspection board works effectively;
- *Community investment supervision board*: commune has a community investment supervision board; community investment supervision board effective.

The change of vertical accountability in Vietnam since 2011 can be seen in Table 9.

Table 9. Overall trend of vertical accountability in Vietnam

Subdimensions	Scale (min)	Scale (max)	2011	2012	2013	2014	2015
Interactions with local authorities	0.33	3.3	1.87	1.88	1.78	1.85	1.83
People's inspection boards	0.33	3.3	1.85	1.87	1.97	1.94	1.78
Community investment boards	0.34	3.4	1.78	1.83	1.90	1.94	1.85

Source: CECODES et al. 2016

Interactions with local authorities seem to follow the cycle of a year up, then a year down since 2011, whereas the value of the indicators of people's inspection boards and community investment board continually increased in the four years from 2011 through 2014, then dropped in 2015. These two subdimensions play an important role in supervising the efficiency of the local government or the governance in Vietnam. As the data in Figure 3 and Table 9 show, there has recently been a decrease in the interaction efficiency between government and citizens.

Anti-corruption in the public sphere

The control of corruption is the fourth dimensions in the PAPI's research on local people experiences with local governance. This dimension includes four main subdimensions with twelve indicators:

- **Limits of public sector corruption:** No diverting of public funds; no bribes for land title; and no kickbacks for construction permits.
- **Limits on corruption in service delivery:** no bribes at public district hospitals; and no bribes for teacher favoritism.
- **Equity in State employment:** no bribes for State employment; no relationship for State employment.
- **Willingness to fight corruption:** know the anti-corruption law; provinces serious about combating corruption; denunciation of prices; and victims denuciate bribes request.

These subdimensions have been changing over the period of 2011–2015 as indicated in Table 10.

Table 10. **Overall Trend of Fighting Corruption**

Subdimensions	Scale (min)	Scale (max)	2011	2012	2013	2014	2015
Limits of public sector corruption	0.25	2.5	1.40	1.44	1.56	1.53	1.39
Limits on corruption in service delivery	0.25	2.5	1.76	1.75	1.83	1.81	1.75
Equity in employment	0.25	2.5	0.94	0.96	1.02	0.99	0.92
Willingness to fight corruption	0.25	2.5	1.66	1.75	1.74	1.78	1.69

Sources: Recalculated from PAPI reports from 2011 to 2015; CECODES et al. 2016)

A significant drop can be seen in 2015 for all subdimensions, especially the local responses to the first three subdimensions with the lowest scores. These responses are below the median, presenting the current difficulties controlling corruption in the local government in Vietnam. Findings from the 2015 report also show the decline in citizen willingness to fight corruption (as the percentage of bribe victims reporting the bribe-taking acts), which presents 9.15 percent in 2011, then decreases to 7.01 percent in 2012, and 2.9 percent, 2.96 percent, and 2.67 percent in 2013, 2014, and 2015, respectively.

Public administrative procedures

This dimension implies the quality of public administrative services in the locals important to citizens. It includes certification services as well as application procedures for construction permits, land use rights certificates, and personal documents. In particular, this dimension looks at how professional and responsive administrative services provided are. There are eight indicators used to measure this dimension, grouped into Certification procedures; Construction permits; Land procedures; and Personnel procedures. These indicators are (a) the clarity of application procedures, (b) publicity of application fee; (c) competence of civil servants, (d) behavior of civil servants, (e) reasonable paperwork load, (f) notification of deadlines, (g) receipt of results within the set deadline, and (h) overall service satisfaction.

Table 11. **Overall Trend of Public Administrative Procedures**

Subdimensions	Scale (min)	Scale (max)	2011	2012	2013	2014	2015
Certification procedures	0.25	2.5	1.68	1.67	1.69	1.71	1.59
Construction permits	0.25	2.5	1.77	1.77	1.76	1.75	1.75
Land procedures	0.25	2.5	1.58	1.57	1.58	1.55	1.55
Personnel procedures	0.25	2.5	1.84	1.86	1.85	1.86	1.86

Source: CECODES et al. 2016

Citizen satisfactions with the subdimensions of construction permits, land procedures, and personal procedures seem to be stable, while such responses to certification procedures are slightly dropped in 2015. As shown in the overall trend, it can be seen that the public administration procedure is at the above-middle range of responses on the form of good governance in Vietnam.

Public Service Delivery

This dimension looks at four public services comprising health care, primary education, basic infrastructure, and residential law and order. The whole period 2011–2015 witnessed a stable increase in the citizen satisfaction on this dimension.

The four subdimensions include sixteen indicators as follows:

- **Public health:** population with health insurance; quality of health insurance; quality of free medical care for children; poor households are subsidized; checks for children are free; total hospital quality.
- **Public education:** kilometer walk to school; number of minutes traveling to school; total school quality.
- **Infrastructure:** quality of roads; frequency of garbage pickup; sharing drinking tap water; sharing drinking unclean water.
- **Law and order:** how safe is locality; change in safety over time; crime rate in locality.

The changes in these subdimensions are presented in Table 12.

Table 12. Overall Trend of Public Service Delivery

Subdimensions	Scale (min)	Scale (max)	2011	2012	2013	2014	2015
Public health	0.25	2.5	1.75	1.78	1.78	1.80	1.75
Public education	0.25	2.5	1.65	1.67	1.68	1.66	1.68
Basic infrastructure	0.25	2.5	1.75	1.85	1.86	1.92	1.98
Law and order	0.25	2.5	1.60	1.60	1.62	1.64	1.64

Sources: Recalculated from PAPI reports from 2011 to 2015; CECODES et al. 2016

Among the public services, high responses about citizen satisfaction focus on the basic infrastructure. Vietnam experienced significant improvements in the basic infrastructure in last few decades, which are easily seen nationwide from the road systems to the educational and residential buildings. The law and order subdimension got the lowest responses. Public health got the second highest responses by the citizens. It started with the highest responses (same as the score for basic infrastructure) in 2011 and continually increased to the peak in 2014 then slightly dropped in 2015. Overall, public service delivery has seen a constant increase for the whole period 2011–2015; it is the sole dimension to receive the mean of citizen satisfaction responses above 7 on a 10-point scale. Public service delivery is most clear on constructing the good governance in Vietnam.

Responses for Improving Governance

Efforts on Improving the National Public Administration

Being aware of the role of public administration in the social development of the early 2000s, while Vietnam was an active member of the global association and membership, Vietnam's prime minister approved the Decision on the Public Administration Reform for 2001–2010, No. 136/2001/QĐ-TTG, in 2001. This reform agenda consists of four main directions: (a) reform of institutions, (b) reform of the public administration system, (c) improvement of qualifications for public servants, and (d) reform of public finance. Overall, this reform aims to (a) reduce the number of public servants, (b) make clear the functions and roles of government management in the market economy, (c) promote the transformation administrative style from more bureaucratic-based to a modernized management model that is compatible with a market economy, (d) boost the division of the administrative system with priority given to the empowerment of the local government, (e) have the socialized directions on public services, improvement of public administrative procedures, to have a one-stop administrative system to provide good services for citizens and enterprises, (f) to have higher qualified public servants (Acuna-Alfaro 2009).

A report in 2004 by the funders of social development in Vietnam showed that the country achieved significant outcomes in transforming its public administrative system, with modernization and good governance approach (Acuna-Alfaro 2009). However, this report also pointed out the weakness caused by the consequences of the long period of bureaucracy in Vietnam, such as short-term financial distribution and planning, with no clear indicators for the efforts of administrative systems. The government still played a deep role in production and service delivery of many social aspects. There is less transparency in public administration, the weakness of authority delivery system and state property management, and the inefficacy of public administration reform in Vietnam as well. In addition, anti-corruption activities in Vietnam are still limited and unsuccessful.

At the Eleventh Communist Party Congress in 2011, the Party stated that the ideas for economic and social transformation and the leadership style had been slowly transformed, which was not compatible with the national development; there was also a prominent "achievement disease"; poorly-designed and strict legal system; poor state management; burden on the state system in that there is a significant sector of government staff who are less qualified in skills and attitudes; the implementation of the state system is less efficient in dealing with critical social problems and urgent social problems; the rights of citizens are not well protected and promoted; corruption and system waste still existed (Vietnam Communist Party 2011). In 2012, the Party also approved the Decree on the urgent problems of contemporary Party development, with more emphasis on administrative weakness (Vietnam Communist Party 2012). In its Twelfth Congress, the Party also stated that the role of state administration is still limited, especially in terms of anti-corruption, welfare, and local participation in the national policy-making process (Vietnam Communist Party 2016).

Henceforth, the Government issued a comprehensive strategy on public administrative reform (2011 and 2014) and the Decision to reduce servants and staff in the public administrative system (2014). The latter decision aims at having better governance and administration in Vietnam. This comprehensive strategy, as the next step from the first scheme, includes many urgent activities and required actions to have a simple, transparent, and supported administrative units, and they are able to meet the all local people demands. This strategy aims to:

(a) construct and complete the institutional system with a market-oriented economy in order to liberate the productive forces and mobilize and use effectively all resources for national development;

(b) create a fair business environment that is liberal, facilitated, and transparent in order to minimize the costs of time and funds of enterprises of all economic sectors in compliance with administrative procedures;

(c) develop a system of state administrative agencies from the central to grassroots level that is smooth, clean, strong, modern, effective, and efficient to enhance democracy and the rule of law in operation of Government and state administrative units;

(d) ensure the implementation of democratic rights for all, protection of human rights, and attachment of human rights to the national interests;

(e) develop better officials and public servants with high qualifications and competence, who meet the requirements to serve the people and to the country's development. (Vietnamese Government 2011)

The main focuses of administrative reform in the next ten-year period are institutionalized reform; constructing and improving the quality of the official and public servants; emphasizing the wage policy reform to create real motivation for officials and to help public servants to perform civic services with high quality and efficiency; to improve the quality of administrative services and the quality of public services.

Efforts on Anti-corruption

In addition to many initiatives on developing and implementing the programs and activities to enhance the role of the administrative system, the government of Vietnam also makes efforts to solve the critical problem of corruption. Recent research in Vietnam has confirmed that the nature and extent of the problem of corruption is varied and multidimensional, presenting in many fields and sizes: public or private, small and large. Corruption in Vietnam, as in many other countries, presents in different levels and sectors, and it belongs to the system. This situation shows that there is lack of a system and mechanism to control and prevent corruption. The notion of corruption is considered according to the following aspects: regarding the public authority as a tool for personal enrichment (which is expressed as the problems in running for position); caring for personal patronage networks rather than striving for the public interest (identified as caring and supporting those directly related to or to patronage networks of individuals which are considered and consistent to the local culture); taking advantage of the shortcomings and lack of clarification in the regulations as tools in the exercise of power (especially when Vietnamese legal provisions are overlapping and uncover for all the issues).

In 2009, the Government approved the National Strategy for Corruption Prevention to 2020 (Resolution 21/2009/NQ-CP, dated December 5, 2009), which pointed out five groups of measures: (a) strengthening public transparency, (b) public administrative reform;

(c) improving the business environment including the private sector, (d) implementation of state power, and (e) strengthening the role of society and mass media agencies. Items (a), (d) and (e) are the means to implement solutions to the others; this also means that items (b) and (c) are the aims of the Strategy.

Report by Gainsborough et al. (2009) suggested that the actions of the Vietnamese Government have not been effective. However, it already exposes the efforts on raising the social awareness about the role of public administration. The Party and the Government of Vietnam have also taken steps to focus on the problem of corruption; the significant benchmark for this effort was the year of 2005 with the passage of the Anti-Corruption Law.

Specific Efforts by the Local Governments

To date, the PAPI has been seen as a significant tool for the State and local government to make changes for social development and citizen requirements. On the basis of the annual PAPI report, the State and local governments propose action plans to increase the efficiency of the public administration in Vietnam.

As presented in the "Good Governance from the WGI" section, reforming the public administration has been a long-term national strategy. It is very urgent for Vietnam's government while Vietnam joins the ASEAN community and signs the Trans-Pacific Partnership. So, administrative reform would reduce any unexpected barriers for foreign partnerships and for local investment and start-ups.

have created action plans to improve the governance index

and found critical solutions that are based on their conditions and resources. In 2012, the four provinces of DakLak, Kon Tum, QuangNgai and Thai Nguyen issued their directives and resolutions for all provincial agencies to improve the administrative index. In 2013, five provinces (Ca Mau, BinhThuan, Dong Thap, BinhDinh, and DakNong) clearly made action plans following the PAPI report. The number of provinces that issued activities to improve the administrative index increased in 2014 to six (Thai Nguyen, Ha Giang, An Giang, Quang Tri, BacGiang, and Phu Yen).

All efforts and directives by the provincial government aim at constructing a better administration and assign significant tasks to related agencies to improve the efficiency of the governing bodies.

Table 13. Responses by the Can Tho Province to Improve Governance (2015 PAPI)

Overall aims: striving toward a democratic, transparent, and strong administration with effective operations and performance of the government from grassroot levels to serve ordinary people. By 2017, Can Tho will be classified in the group with the highest PAPI index scores. ***Specific aims***: Improving all six subdimensions of PAPI, with specific focus on the following: • Transparency will be increased by 30% in 2017 in compared to 2014, (with the total at 6.57 among 10) • Accountability will be improved by strengthening the tasks of the People Inspection Board and Supervisory Board of Investment, with 30% compared with 2014 (with 6.63 points); • Accelerating the reform of administrative procedures by 20% compared with 2014 (at 7.90 points); • Improving the quality of public service provision with 20% compared with 2014 (at 8.05 points); • Controlling the corruption in the public sector, with a 20% increase in comparison to 2014 (at 7.41 points); • Enhancing the local participation with a 30% increase in comparison to 2014 (at 6.28 points) *Sources:* PAPI.VN; CECODES et al. 2016

Citizen Confidence and Contribution to Constructing Good Governance

Local citizens present their comprehensive perspective on the public administrative in Vietnam. As seen in the "Good Governance in Vietnam: Perspective from Different Indicators" section, the administration in Vietnam (as good governance) seems to have decreased in its values, according to the citizen voices on their experiences. However, the confidence in and contribution to social development is still considerable.

Table 15. **Citizen Confidence in the Government**

Mean (1 = very negative, 100 = very positive)	2010	2011	2012	2013	2014
Confidence in National Assembly	90.43	91.30	89.74	89.97	90.15
Confidence in Central Government	91.08	90.85	88.97	89.33	89.86
Confidence in Province Government	85.47	86.60	86.45	86.80	86.87
Confidence in district government	83.16	84.84	84.78	85.17	85.20
Confidence about commune government	81.51	83.11	83.19	83.70	83.87
Confidence about village head	–	85.16	85.57	86.30	86.00
Confidence about commune police	80.52	82.25	82.78	83.02	83.08
Confidence in the district court	82.50	85.06	85.44	85.62	85.50

Source: Reanalyzed the PAPI data from 2010 to 2014

Overall, the citizen responses on confidence about the government and the living conditions show that citizen confidence in the

National Assembly is the highest in the whole period except the year 2010. Confidence in community police is the lowest of all government bodies constantly. Among the government levels, it was found that the commune government was ranked the lowest one. It seems that direct/local government did not receive responses as high as the higher/indirect governments. However, the village head got responses higher than the confidence in the commune government. In Vietnam, the village head plays an important role in supervising the life of the local people and having close contact with them.

For the whole period, it was found that the year 2012 got the lowest responses regarding the citizen confidence; citizen confidence increased in 2013, and kept that confidence in 2014, except for confidence in the province government, commune government, and district court.

Despite that citizen experience with local administration is just above the average level, their confidence in the governments, police, and court are still positive, which shows that the citizens are still trusting and have confidence in the government; this is a critical signal for citizen participation in social development.

Table 16. Contribution by Local Citizens to Community Development

Characteristics of contribution	2011	2012	2013	2014
Family contributed to build public works	52.8%	46.6%	50.3%	52.6%
Forms of contribution				
Money contribution	93.1	91.6	93.0	93.7
Labor contribution	21.2	23.0	24.4	24.5
In kind contribution	1.9	2.1	1.9	2.1
How to contribute				

Requested by village head	21.1	20.6	24.0	29.8
Requested by local authorities	24.9	29.2	30.1	27.4
Voluntary	54.0	49.6	46.0	42.7
Participation in making decisions for public works	50.9	49.9	55.8	60.7
Participation in contribution to public work design	30.1	29.7	33.9	35.7

Around 50 percent of citizens in this research reported their family contribution to the public works. For the period of 2011–2014, there is a small drop in 2012, then a stable increase from 2012–2014. The same trend also happens with regard to the form of monetary contribution. The labor contributions seem to continually increase for the whole period. It also can be seen that family contributions requested by the village head goes up, whereas the voluntary form of that contribution goes down. In addition, there is a clear improvement of citizen participation in decision making and design of public works for the years 2012–2014.

Monetary contribution is prominent in the form of contributions to the public works, whereas citizens' voluntary contributions seem to decrease.

Discussion and Conclusions

Good governance is not clearly stated in Vietnamese contexts, where the term has been used interchangeably with *public administration*. It needs more research in the social sciences approach, especially from the perspective of political sciences.

Good governance from the current indexes (i.e., WGI, PCI, CPI, and PAPI) show that efforts by the State to improve governance and administration in Vietnam are compatible with the worldwide indicators for good governance. Implications from the PAPI, PCI, and CPI, which were developed and constructed socially in Vietnamese condition, are important for policy makers and social researchers related to public administration and governance in Vietnam.

The content and index of governance implied from the PAPI also makes significant impacts on social development in Vietnam, given that a large number of citizens who participated in this survey show their voices and these voices are listened and presented in the reports. In addition, the local governments have proposed their action plan to promote annual indicator(s) of public administration. These efforts, from the citizens and government, would shift the whole governing process toward the better outcomes. Governances, as referred to in the PAPI reports, would show that the efficiency of governance in Vietnam is not good enough from the voices of the citizen expectations.

On looking at the period of 2011–2015, which is the whole term of the Government, National Assembly, and local government, it is clearly seen that governance seems to have decreased by the end of the period. This also implies that the governing bodies express their policies and action plan better than they deliver the practical activities. Among the subdimensions of good governance in

Vietnam, transparency and accountability are quite low according to citizens' responses, which present the situation of lacking the critical implications for constructing good governance in Vietnam. These aspects should be highly considered as the foci to be improved for social development purpose. These findings are compatible with the current indexes WGI and CPI worldwide on presenting ideas about the efficiency of governance in Vietnam. So, the internal and external perspectives of good governance in Vietnam are consistent.

The reports about the public administration index have been widely published and introduced in Vietnam, which also helps the local citizens to believe that their voices about the public administration have been heard and included. This situation would involve and attract more voices and participation by citizens on constructing good governance in Vietnam, and contributing to social development, improving the trust in government as well.

The term *good governance* is still not well defined in the Vietnamese context, which needs further consideration and specific research from an interdisciplinary perspective. Suggestions for making better governance will be comprehensive approach: the central governance focuses more on adjusting the legal, policies and mechanism for the whole nation, while the local governance emphases more on economic renovation, so the combination of PAPI and PCI in Vietnam is socially constructed to improve governance.

Some further ideas and suggestions on making good governance in Vietnam:

• The three words *Independence*, *Freedom*, and *Happiness*, currently stated in the Constitution, should be included in all national action plans and strategies that are seen as the objectives of good governance in Vietnam;

- Maximizing the international cooperation and localizing all the environmental conditions for such cooperation and investment;
- Good relationships and contacts from citizens to society to state and the world, on the basis of the mutual benefits, transparency, accountability. and responsibility;
- Having the strategic development perspective in the coming years in terms of combining the national strengths that are based on the ideas of Nation (with all advances in institutions and civilization to be well globalized), Ethnicity (respecting the cultural core values and harmonizing all ethnic groups), and Country identity; having the combination on economic, politic and military strengths for the international affairs; and improving the social institutions with active citizen participation.
- Actively working on anti-corruption and social problems, by constructing the transparent governmental bodies and the role of the political party; expanding democracy in all aspects of social life; and strengthening the international partnerships in terms of education, health care, transportation, and rural development; dealing with any restriction.
- The form of a state belonging to the people, for the people, and by the people will be the main direction for the

construction of good governance in Vietnam.

Good governance in Vietnam should be constructed to identify the role, function, responsibility, and authority of Government in the closed relationship with Party, market, civil society, and citizens. All activities, such as public administration reform, and improvement of legislation, institutions, follow the direction of having good governance in Vietnam. Among these activities, anti-corruption and transparency are critical and should be promoted because their lack is a significant barrier to social development and motivation for foreign partnerships and the participation of local people.

References

Acuna-Alfaro, Jairo. 2009. *Reforming Public Administration in Vietnam: Current Situation and Recommendations*. Hanoi: Political Publishing House.

Agera, Sam. 2000. *Promoting Good Governance Principles, Practices and Perspectives*, New York: Commonwealth Secretariat.

Agnafors, Marcus. 2013. "Quality of Government: Toward a More Complex Definition." *American Political Review* 107 (3): 433-447.

Berger, P., and T. Luckmann. 1966. *The Social Construction of Reality*. New York: Doubleday.

CECODES, VFF, and UNDP. 2016. PAPI 2015 *Chỉ số hiệu quả quản trị và hành chính công cấp tỉnh ở Việt Nam: Đo lường từ kinh nghiệm thực tiễn của người dân*, NXB Lao động, Hà Nội.

Commonwealth Association of Public Administration and Management. 1995. *Governance in transition: A new paradigm in public administration: A report on the Conference held in Prince Edward Island, Canada, August 28–31, 1994,* Accessed on 10th April 2016 at <http://www.channelingreality.com/Reinvention/CAPAM_A_New_Paradigm.pdf>

Crotty, M. 1998. *The foundations of Social Research: Meaning and Perspective in the Research Process,* London: Sage Publication.

Farazmand, A. 2004. Sound Governance in the Age of Globalization. In *Sound Governance: Policy and Administrative Innovations*, edited by A. Farazmand (pp. 1-24). Westport, CT: Praeger.

Franklin, C. 1995. "Expanding the Vision of the Social Constructionist

Debates: Creating Relevance for Practitioners," *Families in Society: The Journal of Contemporary Human Services* 76 (7): 395-407.

Gainsborough, M., N. D. Dang, and T. P. Tran. 2009. "Corruption, Public Administration and Development: Challenges and Opportunities." In *Public Administration Reform and Anti-Corruption: A Series of Policy Discussion Papers.* Hanoi: United Nations Development Programme.

Given, Lisa M. 2008. *The Sage Encyclopedia of Qualitative Research Methods*. Thousand Oaks, CA: Sage Publications.

Graham, John, Bruce Amos, and Tim Plumptre. 2003. *Principles for Good Governance in the 21st Century: Policy Brief No. 15.* Institute on Governance, Ottawa, Canada. Accessed January 10 2016 at http://unpan1.un.org/intradoc/groups/public/documents/UNPAN/UNPAN011842.pdf.

Grindle M. S. 2007. "Good Enough Governance Revisited." *Development Policy Review.* 25 (5): 553–574.

Harris, S. R. 2010. *What Is Constructionism? Navigating Its Use in Sociology*. London: Sage Publications.

Hồ Chí Minh. 2000a. *Toàn tập: tập 4*. Hà Nội: Nhà xuất bản Chính trị quốc gia,.

Hồ Chí Minh. 2000b. *Toàn tập: tập 7*. Hà Nội: Nhà xuất bản Chính trị quốc gia.

Hồ Chí Minh. 2000c. *Toàn tập: tập 9*. Hà Nội: Nhà xuất bản Chính trị quốc gia.

Holstein, J. A., and G. Miller. 1993. *Reconsidering Social Constructionism: Debates in Social Problem Theory.* Piscataway, NJ: Transaction Publishers.

Hosking, D. M. 1999. "Social Construction as Process: Some New Possibilities for Research and Development." *Concepts & Transformation* 4 (2): 117-132.

Kham, T. V. 2013. "Overview of Social Constructionism and its Potential Applications for Social Work Education and Research in Vietnam. Vietnam National University-Hanoi. VNU *Journal of Social Sciences* 29 (4): 30–37.

Jamil, Ishtiak, Steinar Askvik, and Tek Nath Dhakal, eds. 2016. *In Search of Better Governance in South Asia and Beyond*, pp. 13-14. Singapore: Springer.

Lock, A., and T. Strong. 2010. *Social Constructionism: Sources and Stirrings in Theory and Practice* New York: Cambridge University Press.

Pierre J., and G. B. Peters. 2000. *Governance, Politics and the State.* New York: Macmillan.

Rogers, P., and D. Pilgrim. 2005. *A Sociology of Mental Health and Illness*. Glasgow: Open University Press.

Vietnam Communist Party. 2011. *Văn kiện Đại hội Đảng Cộng sản Việt Nam lần thứ XI.* Accessed on February 10, 2016 at http://chinhphu.vn/portal/page/portal/chinhphu/NuocCHXHCNVietNam/ThongTinTongHop/noidungvankiendaihoidang?categoryId=10000716&articleId=10038382.

Vietnam Communist Party. 2016. *Văn kiện Đại hội Đảng cộng sản Việt Nam lần thứ 12.* Accessed on February 10, 2016. http://daihoi12.dangcongsan.vn/.

Vietnam Government. 2011. *Decision on Approving the National Action Plan on Public Administration from 2011–2020.* Accessed on 15th February 2016 at http://thuvienphapluat.vn/

van-ban/Bo-may-hanh-chinh/Nghi-quyet-30c-NQ-CP-Chuong-trinh-tong-the-cai-cach-hanh-chinh-nha-nuoc-131576.aspx.

Yu, Keping. 1999. "Introduction to Governance and Good Governance." *Marxism and Reality* 5: 37–41.

Vietnam National Assembly. 1946. *Hiến pháp nước Việt Nam dân chủ cộng hòa,* Accessed on 16th February 2016 at http://moj.gov.vn/vbpq/lists/vn%20bn%20php%20lut/view_detail.aspx?itemid=536

Zhenglai, Deng, and Sujian Guo. 2011. China's Search for Good Governance. New York: Palgrave MacMillan.

Worldbank. 2016. Worldwide Governance Index, Accessed on 17th February 2016 at http://info.worldbank.org/governance/wgi/index.aspx#home

SUARAM. 2015. *Human Rights Report 2015 Overview: Civil and Political Rights*. Petaling Jaya: Suara Inisiatif Sdn Bhd.

SUHAKAM. 2013. *SUHAKAM Annual Report 2012.* Kuala Lumpur: Human Rights Commission of Malaysia.

SUHAKAM. 2015. *SUHAKAM Annual Report 2014.* Kuala Lumpur: Human Rights Commission of Malaysia.

Tam, Weng Wah. 2010. "PCB Performs Similar Function as Ombudsman." *Malaysiakini*, March 22. Accessed April 16, 2016. https://www.malaysiakini.com/letters/127210.

Tavanti, Marco, and Agata Stachowicz-Stanusch, eds. 2013. "Anti-Corruption for Human Security." *The International Journal of Sustainable Human Security* 1 (1): 1–177.

Teh, Benny Cheng Guan, ed. 2012. *Human Security: Securing East Asia's Future*. Dordrecht: Springer.

Teoh, Shannon. 2016. "Malaysia's Attorney-General Clears Najib of Corruption over Cash Gifts from Saudi Royals." *The Straits Times*, January 27.

The Economist. 2015. "Malaysia's Masses Protest against Corruption." August 30.

The Guardian. 2016. "Independent Malaysian News Site Closes Amid Government Clampdown on Media." March 15.

The Star. 2014. "NFC—A Four-Year Scandal Comes to a Head." November 6.

The Sun Daily. 2014. "Court Orders Lift of Ban on Cartoonist Zunar's Two Books." October 9.

Theophilus, Claudia. 2008. "Malaysia Poll Battle Goes Online." *Aljazeera*, March 9.

Transparency International–Malaysia. 2014. "Give MACC Prosecution

Power." *Malaysiakini*, February 5. Accessed April 14, 2016. https://www.malaysiakini.com/letters/253579.

Ugaz, Jose. 2015. "Who Paid the Money and Why?" Speech Presented at the 16th International Anti-Corruption Conference, Putrajaya, Malaysia, September 2. Accessed April 9, 2016. http://www.transparency.org/news/speech/who_paid_the_money_and_why.

Wolfowitz, Paul. 2006. "Good Governance and Development—A Time for Action." Speech at a conference, Jakarta, Indonesia, April 11. Accessed April 18, 2016. http://go.worldbank.org/BEUNCNX0D0.

Woon, Leven. 2013. "High Tolerance for Graft among Chinese." *Free Malaysia Today*, December 28. Accessed April 8, 2016. http://www.freemalaysiatoday.com/category/nation/2013/12/28/high-tolerance-for-graft-among-chinese/.

Yoon, Szu-Mae. 2003. "TI: Nation Found Wanting in Tackling Corruption." *Malaysiakini*, September 18. Accessed April 14, 2016. https://www.malaysiakini.com/news/17115.

4

Democratic Transition and It's Discontents: The Case of Indonesia

Abdul Malik Gismar
Paramadina University, Indonesia

Introduction

The prophetic words of Dankwart Rustow (1970) come to mind when we look at the trend of global democratic transitions: More than 40 years ago, he suggested that "*the factors that keep a democracy stable may not be the ones that brought it into existence.*" Today, despite the new wave of democratization in the Arab world, comparative measures of global democracy show that countries embarking on democratic transition earlier are experiencing a decline in the quality of their democracy. Indeed, after the noise of democratic transition recedes, the painstaking process of delivering the promises of democracy begins. This process does not always run smoothly. On the contrary, it is often arrested, taken on a detour, or even reversed. As a result, ten or fifteen years after the beginning of the transition process, countries may end up in a very different situation from the euphoric expectations at the beginning of the transition. Democracy comes to offer legitimacy for the state, specifically through the establishment of democratic institutions such as multiparty competition, elections, and free press. However, this is not sufficient to guarantee the emergence of a stable democratic state. What, then, is needed to create a stable and flourishing democracy?

In the wake of this trend, pushed by academics across many disciplines, international development agencies, and civil activists, the idea of good government and/or good governance finds it place. A plethora of works has been produced that both philosophically and empirically highlight the necessity of "good government" or "good governance." Depending on who did it (academics, international development agencies, or civil activists), the emphasis and definitions may vary but usually fall anywhere along the spectrum of legitimacy and effectiveness of government, within which issues of social justice, human rights, rule of law, elections, accountability, transparency, and efficiency are expressed.[1] Hence, it is inevitable that the idea of "good" government or governance in these many studies also varies.

This chapter looks into what ideas of good governance might actually emerge or at least be suggested when examining a country in the middle of democratic transition. Indonesia is such a country; fifteen years after embarking on the path of democratic transition and building working democratic governance, how does the picture look? For that purpose, this chapter will concentrate more

1 See Goran Hyden (2012) for a comprehensive review of the concept of governance.

on describing a phenomenon of democratic practice, rather than a complete exposition of a concept or theory of government and/or governance. To do that, first, this chapter will briefly describe the democratic transition in Indonesia, highlighting some of the important demands of democratic reform. It will then describe the Indonesia Democracy Index as the instrument to assess democracy in Indonesia, followed by a description of the dynamic of democratic practice in Indonesia for the past six years as captured through the lens of the Indonesia Democracy Index (2009–2014).[2] In conclusion, this chapter will draw some insights pertaining to what good government or governance might entail.[3]

Indonesia Democratic Transition and Its Demand

Reformasi 1998—the democratic movement that toppled

2 The Indonesia Democracy Index was initiated by the National Planning Agency, with support from the United Nations Development Programme. It has the practical goal of providing a framework to assess and monitor the goals and targets of national and local political development plans. As such, it consciously focuses its operational definitions and indicators more on issues directly related to political affairs than on general and wider issues of government or governance. Hence, it does not, for example, include indicators of economic performance or public services. In developing the index, the National Planning Agency was assisted by a panel of five social and political scientists. The panel was tasked with defining the concept, methodology, and instrument. The writer is a member of the expert panel.

3 I would like to thank Tanno Kamilau Hellau and Edi Waryono for preparing some data for this paper.

President Suharto—has transformed Indonesians' collective consciousness, to borrow from Robert Jay Lifton (1993), from a state of "psychic numbing" characterized by apathy, inaction, and withdrawal as a result of living too long in an oppressive atmosphere, to a free-spirited and enthusiastic psychological state that allows ordinary citizens to hope for a better Indonesia. *Reformasi 1998* was a psychological revolution that brought nothing less than a citizen awakening (Gismar, 2010).

In the new atmosphere of freedom, the relationship between state and society also takes on a new meaning. In Suharto's Indonesia, implied in the word *pemerintah* (the equivalent word for government; it literally means "one who gives orders") and *memerintah* (the equivalent word for governing; it literally means "to give orders") was the idea that the state is free to do anything. The argument given by the government for this free hand is that the state is always impartial and interested only in the politics of the public good and ensuring people's welfare.[4] Indonesians were all too familiar with the fact that in practice, as they experienced during Suharto's regime, even if it was in the pursuit of what it saw as

4 It is interesting that impartiality is almost always assumed to be a characteristic of the state, even in theories of democracies. As Yasmin Dawood (2013) asserts, "most (if not all) theories of democracy describes the state as an impartial institution that acts on behalf of the whole." Even today impartiality is seen to be one of the most, if not the most, important criterion of good government. Even in advanced democracies, the transformation from political party to state is a problematic one. See Rothstein (2011), who argues for impartiality as the core quality of good governance. See also Agnafors (2013) for a discussion of this issue.

national interest, the state could trample over the rights, needs, and wants of its citizens. In post-Suharto Indonesia, the distrust toward government after the three-decade rule of an authoritarian regime is deep, and such assumption and practice are no longer acceptable. As much as the citizens need to be protected by the government, they also need protection against the government's abuse of power.[5]

Hence, in the context of democratic transition in Indonesia, the shift in terminology from *government* to *governance* also carries a profound shift in meaning in the public discourse on public or governmental affairs. The word *tatakelola pemerintahan*, which fits rather well with the term *governance*, is used to substitute for the word *pemerintah* or *government* due to this fundamental shift in the way citizens look at the relation between state and society, as mentioned in the beginning of this section. The term *government* is an expression of political aspiration where the anchor of state and public affairs is the state (state centered), whereas *governance* is an expression of political aspiration where the anchor of public affairs is the citizens (citizen centered). There is an acute awareness in this new terminology that the citizens are sacred. In this new collective consciousness, government, once it is elected, is only one actor (albeit a very important one) among other actors such as civil society and the economic/business sector in the arena of

---

5 As early as 1848, John Stuart Mill realized that the state with all its power can be predatory and it is crucial to be able to establish "protection by the government and protection against the government." According to Mill, the latter is the more important because against all other predators there is still a hope of defending oneself.

governance.[6] These actors must collaborate with one another within the constitutional framework to realize the ideal of a good society.[7] To borrow a loose definition from Berggruen and Gardels (2013), "governance is about how the cultural habits, political institutions, and economic system of society can be aligned to deliver the desired good life for its people. Good governance is when these structures combine in a balance that produces effective and sustainable results in the common interest." In other words, good governance requires all actors from the government (executive, legislative, judiciary, and bureaucracy) and society (civil society, economic/business society) to play their respective roles in a concerted effort. At the center of it all is the well-being of the citizens. What is demanded by the shift is an arrangement of living together and a process of public affairs management where not only are political and bureaucratic pathologies such as corruption, collusion, nepotism, and inefficiency eradicated—or at least minimized—but it must also be just, able to guarantee liberty, and serve the well-being of the citizens.

To realize the aforementioned dreams, Indonesia embarked on a major reform of all sectors and at all levels of government. In a move that many call "big bang reform," the constitution was amended, basic political laws were passed, and many institutional

6 Whereas the term *governance* has been around for quite some time and used in various disciplines and development programs with different meaning and emphasis (see Tiihonen 2004 for example), in Indonesia it came into common use and mainly refers to this meaning. From here on, this article will use the term *governance* with this meaning.

7 See Gismar (2010).

reforms were adopted, including establishing freedom of press, implementing direct presidential elections, and promulgating the legislative framework for decentralized governance.

The main purposes of the decentralization laws, such as Law No. 32/2004 and Law No. 33/2004, were to restructure local political institutions, grant fiscal responsibility to local governments, and improve their professionalism, transparency, and efficiency. The laws strengthened the role of public interests groups at the local level (Eckardt and Shah, 2006). The laws also allowed for formation of public interest groups.

This sudden and substantial change represented a challenge for local governments in all thirty-three (now thirty-four) provinces and about 480 (now more than 500) districts and municipalities, which had accrued little experience under the dominance of the central government. Some observers argued that the decision to open up and involve citizens at all levels of the governance process was simply "too much, too soon" (Hidayat, 2007), but at the same time, perhaps it is the only way to regain and establish the legitimacy of the state.[8]

---

8 See an interesting suggestion from Grindle (2010) that "the idea of good governance owes much to the intellectual resurrection of the state as a positive 'player' in economic and political development." I would argue that in the case of Indonesia, the reasoning for bringing the notion of good governance is deeper than just resurrecting the role of the state; it is answering a more fundamental question of state legitimacy and national unity amid a serious threat of disintegration.

Indonesia Democracy Index

The Indonesia Democracy Index is an instrument used to capture annually the state of democracy in Indonesia's provinces.[9] Any attempt to operationalize "democracy" into measurable aspects, variables, and indicators will inevitably be incomplete. The Indonesia Democracy Index consciously decided not to attempt to develop an all-encompassing tool that aimed at assessing every aspect and nuance of democracy but to develop a measure that can assess the most important aspects of democratic realities in a specific place (i.e., Indonesia's provinces), at a specific time, and for specific purposes. Although the aspects of democracy to be assessed by the index are common targets of democratic assessment worldwide, the indicators that capture these aspects are local and tangible, and some are at a behavioral level. The insistence on using indicators at this level of expression is to be able to capture democracy as it is lived by citizens on the street in everyday life.[10]

9 The pilot index was implemented in 2007. The Indonesia Democracy Index 2009 was implemented with significant changes in the number of indicators and in some aspects of the technical calculation of scores. Comparisons between 2007 and the following years is therefore avoided. The 2009 index results are considered as the baseline. Since then, data were collected every year. Because there is a year's delay in the publication of most data, the picture provided by the index is also at least a year behind. A brief description of the concept and indexing methods is instructive to understanding the results.

10 For detailed definitions of concepts and technical notes of the indexing see Indeks Demokrasi Indonesia 2014. All Indeks Demokrasi Indonesia reports from 2009 to 2014 can be found at http://www.idiproject.org.

The Indonesia Democracy Index attempts to capture democracy through its three most important aspects—that is, the *condition of civil liberty*, *fulfillment of political rights,* and *the performance of democratic institution.* Civil liberty is operationally defined as the freedom of citizens and groups of individuals to come together and to associate or organize, to voice their opinions, and to have a belief or faith. It also means freedom from discrimination and from restriction exercised by other(s) or the state. The index captures civil liberty through four variables, namely 1) freedom of assembly and freedom of association; 2) freedom of expression; 3) religious freedom; and 4) freedom from discrimination.

Political rights is elaborated into two variables that capture not only the system and procedures to guarantee that the rights are fulfilled, but also the behavioral expression of the citizens in their participation to monitor public affairs throughout the year.[11] These two variables are 1) the right to vote and the right to be elected in a general election; and 2) political participation in decision making and monitoring. Participation in a political context refers to involvement or engagement in political processes. The form of political participation that is often used in democratic assessment is, of course, the exercise of the right to vote in a general election

11 Compare with Kenneth A. Bollen (1993), who contends that "*political rights exist to the extent that the national government is accountable to the general population and each individual is entitled to participate in the government directly or through representatives*" and Robert Dahl's (1971) five indicators of political rights: the right to cast a vote, the right to compete for public positions, the right to compete for votes, free and fair elections, and policy making based on public votes or inputs.

(usually indicated by voter turnout). The Indonesia Democracy Index, however, also considers another form of participation that is rarely used as an indicator in democratic assessment but is much more meaningful: citizen involvement in public affairs everyday throughout the year. This involvement may occur at all stages of policy making and implementation, from decision making to assessing or evaluating that decision and participation in implementing those decisions.

An institution of democracy is operationally defined as a public institution established to regulate and carry out the activities of the state and/or the government. These institutions may exist within the executive, legislative, and judicial branches of government, as well as independent commission charged with a certain task (i.e., general elections, political parties, the media, and interest groups). The role of institutions of democracy are captured through the following variables: 1) existence of free and fair general elections; 2) the performance of regional parliament; 3) the performance of political parties; 3) the performance of provincial bureaucracy; and 4) an independent judiciary. These variables are further translated into ten indicators for civil liberty, seven for political rights, and eleven for democratic institutions. The complete list of the aspects, variables, and indicators can be seen in Table 1.

For each of the indicators, evidence was found first in newspaper reports and official documents. In each province, one newspaper was selected (the newspaper with the highest readership) to be content analyzed. Official documents include those issued by regional governments and regional parliaments, such as provincial regulations (*Perda*), gubernatorial decrees, and other official documents such as statistics on voters issued by the Regional General Elections Commission. The National Statistics Agency, which has offices in all provinces and districts across Indonesia, was charged with the data collection. Collected data were cleaned and verified (in terms of their agreement with the indicators) in a meticulous process of going through all one by one, involving the expert panel and the National Statistics Agency's team. Once the data sets were cleaned and verified, data were brought up in focus group discussions in each province to be further verified, qualified, and elaborated (in terms of being an accurate depiction of what had really happened). The participants of the discussion are well-informed persons representing all stakeholders in the province. For certain indicators, interviews with such individuals were conducted to further enrich the data.

Table 1. Aspects, Variables, and Indicators of the Indonesia Democracy Index

Civil Liberties	Political Rights	Democratic Institutions
Freedom of assembly of association	**The right to vote and be voted in a general election**	Free and fair elections
Ind 1 - Threat or use of violence by officer(s) which restrict freedom of assembly and freedom of association	Ind 11 - Incidents in which people's right to vote or get elected is restricted	Ind 18 - Incidents that indicate the partiality of Regional General Elections Commissions (KPUD)

Ind 2 - Threat or use of violence by other(s) which inhibit freedom of assembly and freedom of association	Ind 12 - Incidents of lack/shortage of facilities for people with disabilities as a result of which they cannot exercise their rights to vote	Ind 19 - Incidents or reporting of the fraudulent counting of votes
Freedom of expression	Ind 13 - The quality of the fixed list register voters (Daftar Pemilih Tetap –DPT)	The role of provincial parliament
Ind 3 – Threat or use of violence by officer(s) which restricts freedom of expression	Ind 14 – Percentage of eligible voters who actually vote in a general election (voter turnout)	Ind 20 - The amount of budget allocated for education and health per capita
Ind 4 - Threat or use of violence by people which restricts freedom of expression	Ind 15 - Percentage of female provincial parliamentarian (of the total members of provincial parliament)	Ind 21 – Parliamentary initiative in the making of a regulation
Freedom of belief/ faith (freedom of religion)	**Political participation in decision making and monitoring**	Ind 22 - Number of recommendations put forward by DPRD to the executive
Ind 5 - Written rules and regulations which restrict the freedom or require people to practice their religions	Ind 16 - Demonstrations / strikes that turn violent	**The role of political parties**
Ind 6 - Actions or statements by officials which restrict the freedom or require people, to practice their religions	Ind 17 - Complaints on the running of government	Ind 23 - Number of cadre formation activities carried out by political parties which participate in general elections
Ind 7 - Threat or use of violence by a group of people against other related to religious teachings		Ind 24 - Percentage of women in the stewardship of political parties at provincial level
Freedom from discrimination		**The role provincial bureaucracy**

Ind 8 – Discriminatory rules and regulations on the grounds of gender, ethnicity or against vulnerable groups		Ind 25 - the misuse of government facilities by candidates / political parties in legislative general elections
Ind 9 – Discriminatory actions or statements by regional officials (gender, ethnicity, vulnerable groups)		Ind 26 - The involvement of civil servants in political activities of political parties in legislative general elections
Ind 10 - Threats or use of violence by people/society (gender or ethnicity of the victim and/or vulnerable groups)		**The role of independent judiciary**
		Ind 27 - Controversial rulings handed down by judges
		Ind 28 – Controversial terminations of investigations by prosecutors or police

Thus, the Indonesia Democracy Index employs a fourfold data collection method, each in conjunction with the other with the purpose of covering the weakness of each method. The newspaper and document reviews serve to capture incidents as defined by the indicators throughout the year. A newspaper was chosen as a data source because it reports on the life in the province all year long. Of course, the index uses it because those behind the index are convinced that newspapers in Indonesia are free. However, there is still the possibility of biases for many reasons. This is why these data are then verified and enriched in focus group discussions (which usually include the chief editor of another newspaper in the province) and in-depth interviews.

The Indonesian Democracy Index is calculated in three stages. First, the index of each indicator is calculated. Building upon the score of each indicator, the provincial index and overall index (or Indonesia Democracy Index) is calculated. Before the index itself can be calculated, a separate process calculates the weight of each indicator, variable, and aspect. The aspects of civil liberties, political rights, and institutions of democracy make different contributions to democracy in Indonesia. The same is true of the variables and indicators. The index calculates weights using an analytical hierarchy process.

Figure 1. Scheme of Calculation of Final Score of Each Indicator

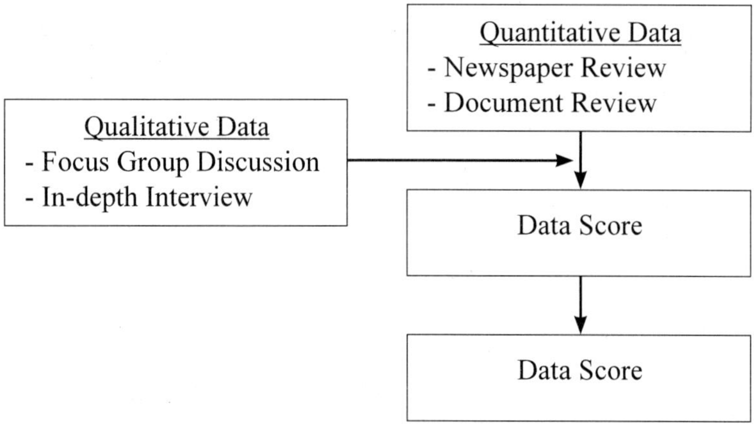

To describe the outcome of democratic performance in each province, a scale of 1 to 100 is used. This scale is a normative scale in which a score of 1 indicates the lowest performance and 100 the highest. The lowest performance is theoretically possible if all the indicators receive the lowest score. The highest performance is theoretically possible if all the indicators receive the highest score.

Democracy in Indonesia: 2009 – 2014

As described in the previous section, the Indonesia Democracy Index is a measure of provincial democracy in Indonesia.12 It produces a democracy index for each province in Indonesia. This chapter will not present the index of all provinces; instead it will present the overall index which is the aggregate of all provinces' democratic performances. As with any aggregation, the overall index is not a description of any province and it is similar to none, but it gives a description of overall trend of Indonesian democratic condition. The disadvantage of seeing Indonesia from this aggregate is that the overall index is missing the uniqueness of each provincial democracy. The advantage, however, is that we are able to see the general pattern and trend for the whole country. For the purpose of this paper and due to space limitations, I have opted to present the aggregate of those provincial indexes instead of presenting all provincial results or one specific province.

The overall trend of democracy in Indonesia for the past six years is depicted in Figure 2. The trend lines depict the three aspects of democracy (the index of each aspect) and the bar graph depicts the aggregate of those three aspects (the overall index). The first thing to note in Figure 2 is that there is a consistent pattern where civil liberty

12 There were thirty-three provinces until 2014. As a result of local reorganizing since 1998, provinces in Indonesia have grown from twenty-seven at the end of the Suharto regime to thirty-four as of 2015.

achieved a high score, indeed a very high score, whereas the other aspects—fulfillment of political rights and the performance of democratic institutions—are trailing behind, rather significantly at times.

Figure 2: Overall Trend of Indonesian Democracy 2009 - 2014

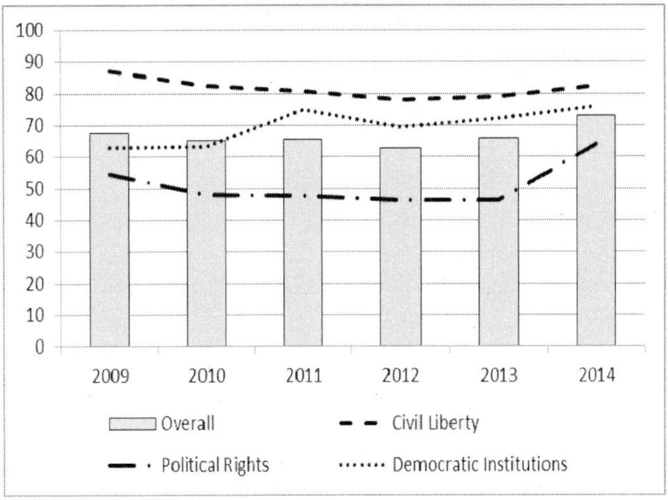

This indicates that in general, the threat to civil liberties in Indonesia is low. There is a real opening up of public spheres, and the rules and regulations established in the post-Suharto era are effective in ensuring that the state does not trample on the civil rights of the citizens. We will also see later (in Indicators 16 and 17) that citizens are also using these open and free public spheres enthusiastically, as evidenced by the public demonstrations occurring daily in every corner of Indonesia. Likewise, the threat of freedom from society, as indicated by incidents where people inhibit or curb others' freedom, is also relatively small.

This finding is, for the most part, in accordance with Freedom House's survey where for many years, they found the condition of civil liberties in Indonesia to be very good and classified the country as "fully free." In 2012, though, Freedom House downgraded Indonesia to "partly free," mainly on the grounds of a very few but high-profile incidents and regulations that limit religious freedom.[13] However, a close look at the conditions of civil liberty from the variables that formed them shows that all variables tend to cluster close to one another at the high scores, except for freedom of expression, which tends to stand alone outside the cluster (significantly so at a lower score). Figure 3 show that in six years all variables of civil liberty scored above 80 except for freedom of expression, which consistently scored lower (as low as 60.86 in 2012).

Figure 3: Civil Liberty Trend 2009 -2014

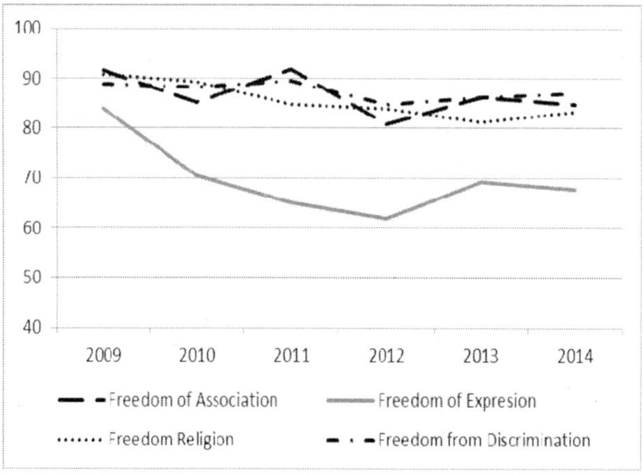

13 Freedom House annually conducts *Freedom in the World Survey*. From 2009 to 2014, Freedom House surveys in Indonesia generally showed more favorable results, especially related to political rights.

This is contrary to the usual image of religious intolerance in Indonesia as the main civil liberty problem. The Indonesia Democracy Index 2009–2014 shows that the tendency to threaten violence, and in many cases to actually resort to violence, exists for many various issues in Indonesia. In 2014 the biggest portion of demonstrations that ended with violence were related to government performance in conducting public affairs. Religious intolerance and tensions certainly occur in Indonesia, and from an ethical standpoint it should be very clear that if one incident occurs in a year, it is already one too many. There is a tendency to attribute the cause of these religious tensions to "primordial" factors (factors within the religion itself) or differences between religions. The remedy, therefore, is to enlighten people, broaden people's religious understanding, or conduct interfaith dialogues to minimize differences and find commonalities between religious values. Although each of these efforts is fine in and of itself, if taken out of context and applied to all cases of religious conflicts and contentions, they could be misleading and counterproductive. Many religious contentions in Indonesia are related to management of religious diversity, rather than to inherent conflicting religious values or deeply rooted religious enmity. One of the most common conflicts between Muslims and Christians in Indonesia, for example, is related to the construction of churches or mosques. Problems occur when Christians wish to build a church in a Muslim-majority area, and vice versa, when Muslims wish to build a mosque in a Christian-majority area. In the constitution of the Republic of Indonesia, the principle is very clear: Every citizen is free to believe in any religion and practice it. Nobody in Indonesia is challenging this constitution. Problems arise when this principle is translated into bad regulations. In the case of mosque or church construction, one regulation that contributes to and exacerbates the tensions is the one prescribing any religious group to ask approval of the residents of the area where they want to construct their house of worship (in the form of certain numbers of signature). This is a very sensitive issue, and it can easily be predicted that approval is very hard to come by if the religion is a minority religion, regardless whether it is Islam or Christianity. This regulation has made it very difficult for Christians to build a church in a predominantly Muslim area and for Muslims to build a mosque in a predominantly Christian area. The problem with this regulation is that it relegates a very sensitive and potentially explosive issue to the street where there is no chance for serious and careful deliberation. This deliberation should happen in the parliamentary chamber, involving all stakeholders. Once a decision that satisfies all group concerns is made, every effort must be made to uphold it.

The picture becomes even more interesting when looking at the trend of each indicator of civil liberty. Table 2 shows trends of all indicators in civil liberty. All indicators in every variable, except for indicators in the freedom of expression variable, tend to have similar scores and show similar trends. Only two indicators consistently obtained scores below 80. Those are "threat or use of violence by officer(s) which restricts freedom of expression" (Indicator 3) and "threat or use of violence by people which restricts freedom of expression" (Indicator

4). Both are indicators of freedom of expression. Of the two, Indicator 4 consistently scores worst. This indicates that in Indonesia today, the threat against freedom of expression from people or society is higher than the threat coming from the state.

Table 2. Conditions of Civil Liberty 2009–2014

<table>
<tr><td>

Freedom of assembly

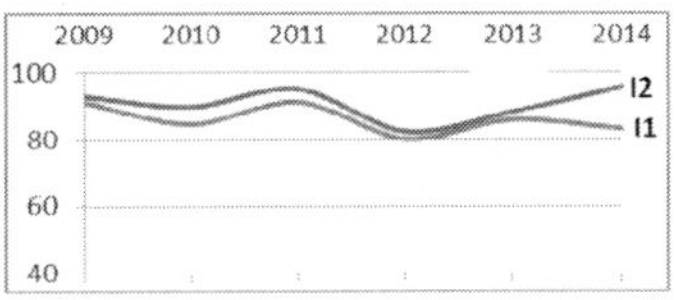

</td><td>

Description of Indicators:

Ind 1 – absence of threat or use of violence from government (assembly)

Ind 2 – absence of threat or use violence from other people/society (assembly)

</td></tr>
<tr><td>

Freedom of Expression

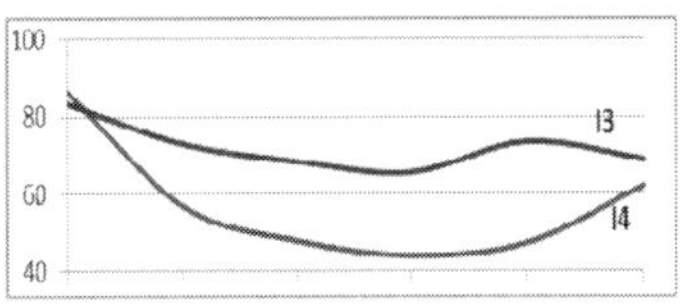

</td><td>

Ind 3 – absence of threat or use of violence from government (expression)

Ind 4 – absence of threat or use of violence from other people/society (expression)

</td></tr>
<tr><td>

Religious Freedom

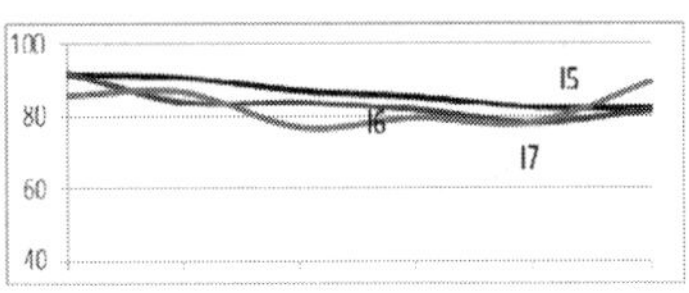

</td><td>

Ind 5 – absence of government rules/ regulation forcing/prohibiting religious practice (religion)

Ind 6 – absence of government actions forcing/prohibiting religious practice (religion)

Ind 7 – absence of threat or use of violence from other people/society (religion)

</td></tr>
<tr><td>

Freedom from discrimination

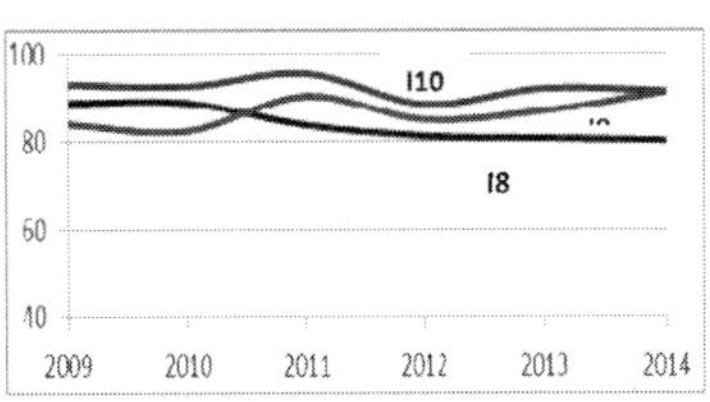

</td><td>

Ind 8 – absence of discriminatory rules based on ethnicity, gender, etc

Ind 9 – absence of discriminatory actions based on ethnicity, gender, etc

Ind 10 – absence of threat of violence by people/society based on ethnicity, gender, etc

</td></tr>
</table>

It is obvious from the trend across the years that freedom of expression in Indonesia has its own dynamic, different from other civil liberty variables. A look at the incidence of violation of freedom of expression suggests that many are associated with political activities in and out of campaign season. Local political activities, especially during election time, are fertile ground for disagreements, tensions, and conflicts; they are obviously partisan and emotionally charged and often find expression that tramples others' freedom of expression.

In contrast to civil liberty, the fulfillment of political rights has consistently scored low in five years. As can be seen from Figure 4, of the two variables in this aspect, in the last year (2014) the score of "the right to vote and get elected" shows a significant jump from the past years. In the meantime, political participation did not move from the previous year's position.

Figure 4: Trend of Political Rights 2009 – 2014

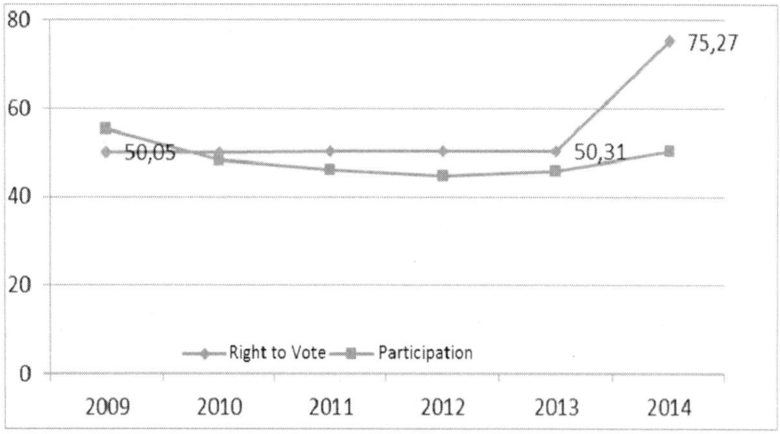

The jump in the "right to vote and be elected" variable is telling an interesting story. The scores of four of the five indicators of this variable are actually similar across the years. Only one indicator, "The quality of the list of eligible voters," jumps drastically in the last assessment. This jump can be attributed almost solely to the success of the Indonesian Election Commission to significantly improve the list of eligible voters. Indeed, in the last round of elections in Indonesia, the Election Commission successfully guaranteed almost all eligible voters that, should they wish to vote, they will be able to vote. This is a major institutional achievement because until 2014 "the list of eligible voters" was a source of never-ending complaints and disputes.

The complexity of the fulfillment of political rights is hidden in the deceivingly simple trend lines. If we disaggregate the political rights variable into its indicators we will see a glimpse of this complexity. Table 3 shows the six-year trends of all indicators. Looking at the variable "the right to vote and be elected," one sees the five indicators seem to fall into three different groupings. The first group consists of indicators with relatively high scores; those are "Incidents in which people's right to vote or get elected is curbed" (Indicator 11) and "voters turn out" (Indicator 14). The second group consists of indicators with low scores; those are "Incidents of lack/shortage of facilities for people with disabilities as a result of which they cannot exercise their rights to vote" (Indicator 12) and "Percentage of female provincial parliamentarians (of the total members of provincial parliament)" (Indicator 15). The third group consists of an indicator with a very low score: "The quality of the list of eligible voters" (Indicator 13).

Table 3. Political Rights Trend 2009–2014

The right to vote and get elected in a general election

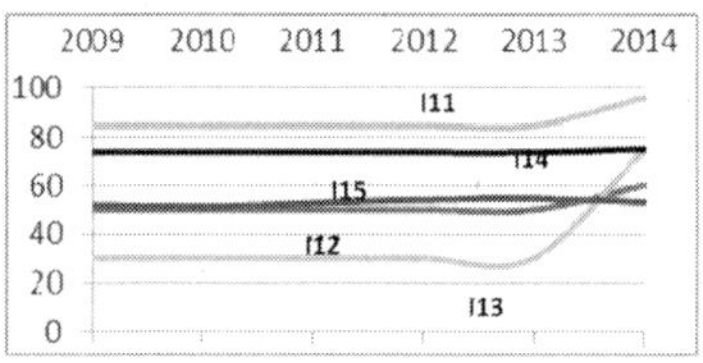

Description of Indicators:

Ind 11 – incidents in which people's right to vote or get elected is curbed

Ind 12 – lack of facilities for people with disabilities (disabled people)

Ind 13 – The quality of the list of voters

Ind 14 – % of eligible voters who vote in a general election (voter turnout)

Ind 15 – % of women elected as members of provincial parliament compared to the total members of provincial parliament

Political participation in decision making and monitoring

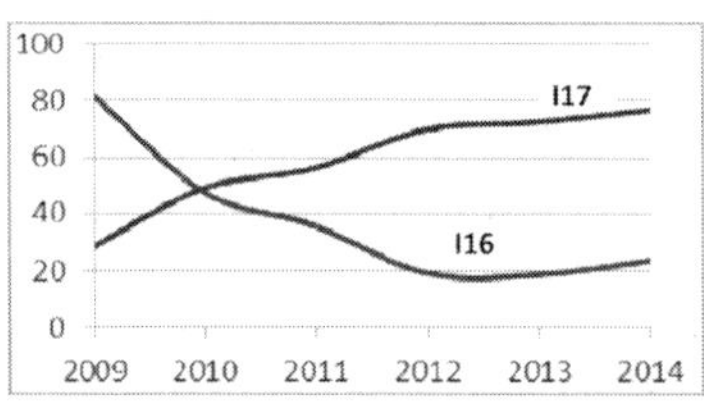

Ind 16 – demonstrations /strikes that end with violent

Ind 17 – number of complaints against the running of public/government affairs

It is important to note that in 2014, three indicators showed improvement in their scores. All of those indicators are related to the performance of institutions charged with the running of general elections. At the same time, indicators related to people's eagerness to vote have been relatively high and stable across the years.

The political participation variable measures two sides of political participation: on one side, people's awareness and participation in public and governmental affairs (Indicator 16), and on the other, how they express their opinions and feelings about it (Indicator 17). The trends in Indicators 16 and 17 show an interesting relationship between the enthusiasm to be involved in public and government affairs (e.g., to monitor, report, protest, demonstrate, strike, boycott) and the civility of the expression. As shown in Table 3, the score of people's participation (Indicator 17) has been increasing for the past six years. This is a good sign that people do care about what is going on around them and are willing to be involved; if they do not like what they see, they will let those responsible know how they feel. This is a good sign of civic involvement, a much-needed prerequisite for a healthy democracy. However, the score of Indicator 16, which specifically measures public demonstrations that end in violence, is going in the opposite direction—it is getting worse by the year. So, although there is more public expression, there is also more violence.

Glances at violent demonstrations clearly show widespread questioning of the state's legitimacy and capability. Figure 5 identifies the issues of the demonstration.

Figure 5. Issues of Demonstrations that Ended in Violence 2014 (Jawa)

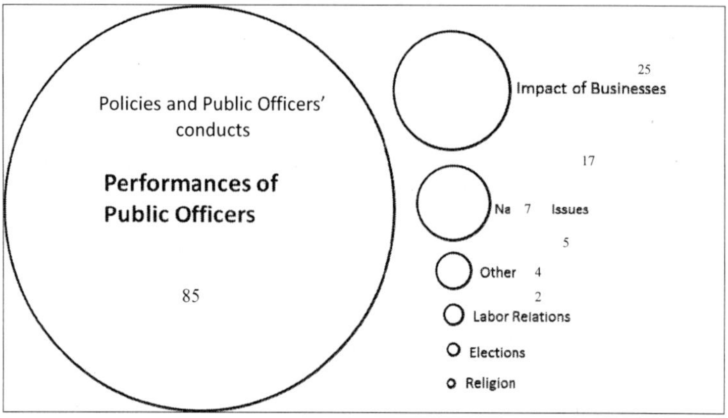

Source: Indonesia Democracy Index 2014, data for indicator 16

With regard to the demonstrations that ended in violence, data from Indonesia Democracy Index 2015 for all provinces on Java Island show that the violence is overwhelmingly targeted at the government, from mundane everyday issues such as unmaintained roads, electricity, clean water, poverty, and health to bigger issues such as corruption, various government policies, and land disputes. The next largest issue is related to labor relations (such as unfair wages, perceived government partiality toward business) and the impact of business activities (such as pollution, destruction of public roads, destruction of the environment, and the like). Surprising perhaps to many people, violent demonstrations related to religious issues constitute only a very small portion of the total number of demonstrations that end in violence.

Who are participating in these demonstrations? Figure 6 gives some indication that anyone can be passionately involved in a demonstration, even one that might end in violence. Demonstration, which used to be the monopoly of college students, is now open to everybody, everywhere.

Figure 6. Participants of Demonstrations that End in Violence 2015 (Jawa)

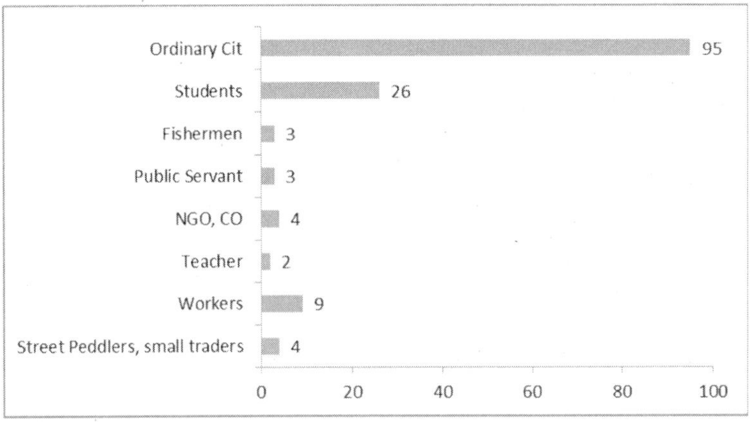

As is clear from Figure 6, those involved in all kinds of demonstrations in Indonesia were, overwhelmingly, ordinary citizens. On one hand, this phenomenon shows a high civic engagement among the citizens, an important ingredient for democracy to flourish. On the other hand, too much of it might also be a sign of widespread discontent with areas of government.

The performance of democratic institutions in the past six years shows the most fluctuation among the three aspects of democracy being assessed. The score goes up and down across the years, but the overall trend is climbing. There is distinct grouping of the variables into the high scoring variables and low scoring ones, as can be seen in Figure 7.

Figure 7. Trend of Democratic Institutions 2009 -2014

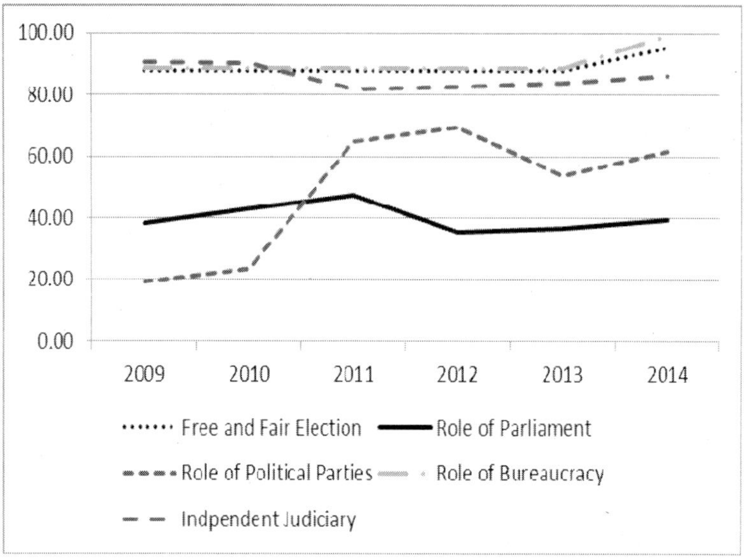

The high scoring variables are free and fair elections, the role of bureaucracy, and role of independent judiciary. These variables consistently scored above 80. On the other hand, the role of parliament and the role of political parties fluctuated in the lowest range of scores and at times almost hit the floor. These two variables drag down the overall performance of democratic institutions and are closely related; the role of the parliament is determined by the role of the political parties through the members they send to the parliament. Table 4 details the scores of each indicator.

Table 4. Conditions of Democratic Institutions 2009–2014

Free and fair elections

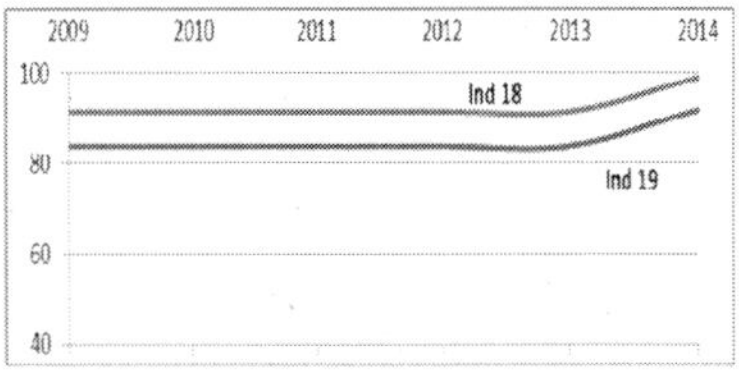

Description of Indicators

Ind 18 – the partiality of Regional General Elections Commissions (KPUD)

Ind 19 – Incidents of fraudulent counting of votes

The role of Parliament

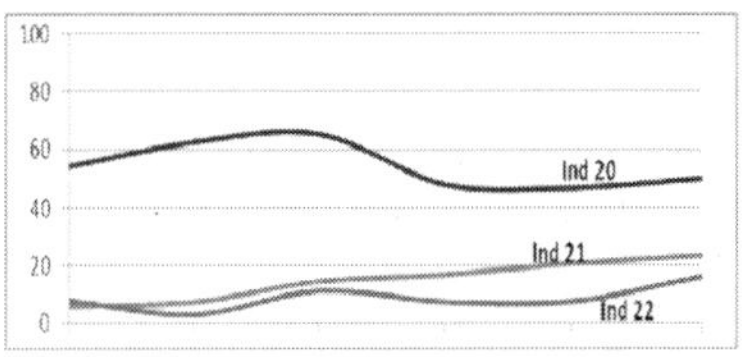

Ind 20 – The amount of budget allocated for education and health per capita

Ind 21 – Parliamentary initiative in the making of a regulation

Ind 22 – Number of recommendations put forward by DPRD to the executive

The role of political parties

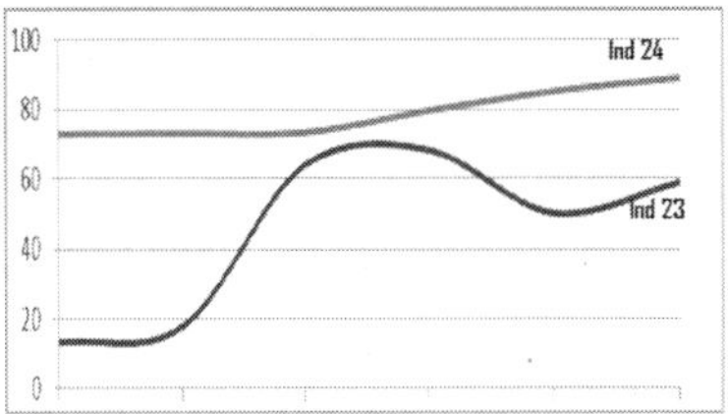

Ind 23 – Number of cadre formation activities carried out by political parties which participate in general elections

Ind 24 – Percentage of women in the stewardship of political parties at provincial level

The role of Bureaucracy

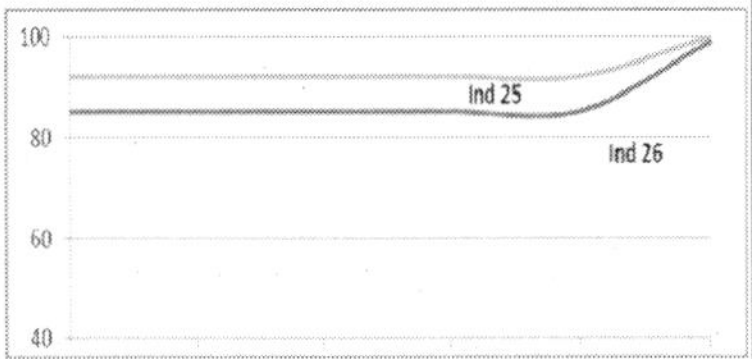

I25 –the misuse of government facilities by candidates /political parties in legislative general elections

I26 – The involvement of civil servants in political activities of political parties in legislative general elections

Independent judiciary 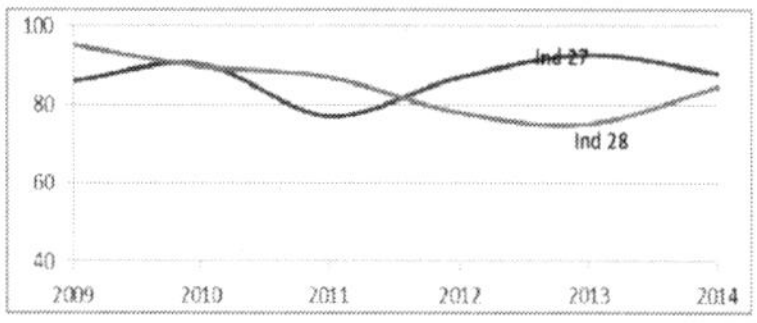	Ind 27 – Controversial rulings handed down by judges Ind 28– Controversial terminations of investigations by prosecutors or police

The most disheartening result of the Indonesia Democracy Index, no doubt, is the performance of the parliament. As Table 4 shows, all indicators for the role of parliament scored extremely low throughout the six-year assessment period. This clearly indicates that the provincial parliament simply did a miserable job as the representative of the citizens. This certainly is related to the performance of political parties, as described earlier. Because the performance of political parties is poor (i.e., unable to attract and educate political cadres), we cannot expect much of the parliament. By sending unqualified people to the parliament, political parties have put a ceiling on what the parliament can achieve.

The discrepancy of performance between the index's aspects of democracy indicates a certain paradox in Indonesian democracy. On the one hand, the room for civil liberty is wide open and the citizens freely and enthusiastically express themselves. On the other hand, Indonesia's democratic institutions are so far behind in capacity and cannot respond adequately to the democratic demands arising from the opening up of civil liberty. Democratic realities in Indonesia and to some degree social life in general, for that matter, were shaped by this paradox. From the villages in the most remote province to the capital city, one can witness enthusiastic public participation in monitoring public and government affairs. These legitimate democratic demands, however, meet with democratic institutions that lack the capacity to adequately respond. The often results in frustration that may find contrasting expression, either apathy or anger; both breed contempt of the state.

Emerging Images of What Good Governance Should Entail

In an earlier section of this chapter I borrowed an understanding of good governance from Berggruen and Gardels (2013), who suggested that "governance is about how the cultural habits, political institutions, and economic system of society can be aligned to deliver the desired good life for its people. Good governance is when these structures combine in a balance that produces effective and sustainable results in the common interest." This is a generic understanding that does not explain the requirements or the conditions for such "alignment" or "combination." The core message, however, is an important one. Berggruen and Gardels seem to suggest the importance of the interplay of the state and society arena or actors in a particular social context and historical juncture to come up with the best possible arrangement to achieve a good society. This is different from the earlier tendency (especially within the international development circle) to find a general or universal theory, propositions, or concepts of good governance.[14]

Although it is not a complete picture, the Indonesia Democracy Index 2009–2014 illustrates some of the complications of thinking about good governance in a democratic transition and suggests some conditions that might be necessary for constructive alignment between state and society's actors to occur. In the following paragraphs, I extrapolate some of its basic insights. The first three relate to government, and the last two relate to society. They are not mutually exclusive. They are also not necessarily new insights, but rather they might corroborate some of the ideas of good governance that have been proposed by others.

1. Good Governance Requires Both Legitimate And Effective Government

When a government is perceived to be illegitimate due to various factors such as impartiality and suppression of civil liberty, such as happened in Suharto's Indonesia, citizens want a change. The most attractive alternative system available to replace it is democracy. Indeed, democracy has a strong appeal to address issues such as liberty and equality (justice, civil rights, human rights). Yet, democracy often is not the most effective way to deliver public

14 See Grindle (2004, 2010), who argues that such a general theory will fail to address important questions in any policy planning such as what is essential and what is not, what should come first and what should follow, what can be achieved in the short term and what can only be achieved over the longer term, and what is feasible and what is not.

services. There was time when, to some international development activists, democracy was seen as a "recipe for weak, unstable governments"; therefore, democracy must wait until certain level of development is achieved before it can be introduced (see Carothers, 2010).

The Indonesia Democracy Index indicates that in today's Indonesia, the bulk of the discontented citizens are dissatisfied with the performance of the state in delivering public services. Their complaints and demonstrations are mainly related to mundane citizens' needs such as clean water, electricity, health, and badly maintained roads. However, this civil discontent may turn into a direct challenge to the authority of the state when concerns are not responded to adequately. When challenges occur, they are often expressed against state apparatuses (civilian and police officers); in some cases, they may even involve attacks on personnel and destruction of offices.

Good governance requires both legitimacy and effectiveness to deliver the promises of democracy. Although one might think that the legitimacy take precedence over the effectiveness, the lack of effectiveness will immediately erode the legitimacy of government.

2. The Relationship Between Legitimacy and Effectiveness Is Not Zero Sum

Legitimacy and effectiveness often are dichotomized and put along the same dimension, creating a a zero-sum relationship. In this relationship, a gain in one aspect must be paid by a loss in the other aspect; effectiveness is achieved at the expense of legitimacy. In the case of Indonesia, there are voices arguing that Indonesia has gone too far in its attempt to be legitimate by allowing unbridled freedom of expression, to the extent that the government is prevented from doing its job.

I would argue that this is not necessarily the case. The relation between the legitimacy of the state and its effectiveness is not a zero-sum relationship but an orthogonal relationship, with each going perpendicularly to different direction. Although the two are interlocked in a systemic relationship, they actually answer separate dimensions of a democratic life. This can be depicted as follows:

Figure 8. Legitimacy - Efficiency Relationship

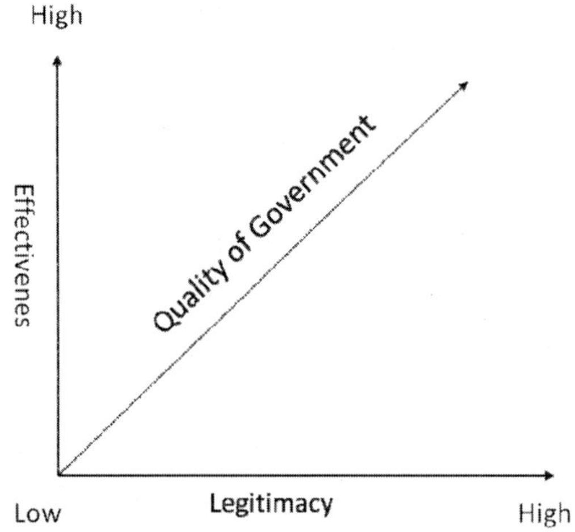

We should be able to imagine a quality of government where the legitimacy of the state is high, and at the same time, its effectiveness is also high. In fact, this would be an ideal government, one that is politically legitimate and at the same time responsive to the needs of the citizens. The opposite of this is a condition where legitimacy is low and the effectiveness of the state is also low, which will create a bad government, one that is not legitimate politically and is unable to provide for the needs of the citizens. Other conditions can also be imagined, where one dimension is high and the other is low. Therefore, from an evaluative perspective, the quality of government at any given time is the coordinate where the level of legitimacy meets the level of effectiveness.

This way of seeing the relationship between legitimacy and effectiveness suggests that at any given historical point, the concern and priority of establishing good governance might be different. Indonesia, for example, at this point of its democratic consolidation, may be falling into relatively moderate to high legitimacy and low to moderate effectiveness. The main issue in terms of legitimacy is a representational problem as a result of low-performing political parties and representative bodies. At this particular time in Indonesia, the concern of good governance should be political parties, the representative bodies, and the state's capacity to respond to citizens' needs and wants.

3. Good Government Requires the Existence of Real Representation

Indonesia has succeeded in establishing all necessary

institutions of democracy. However, discontent abounds and is widespread down to the grassroots level. Democratic institutions are necessary but are not a sufficient condition for a stable democracy. The story emerging from the fulfillment of political rights and the performance of the parliament in Indonesia is that a well-run, regular, free, and fair election does not translate into better representation of the interests of the people. Therefore, whereas the people have the *vote*, they still do not have the *voice*; whereas they are very much engaged with government affairs, this engagement does not bring the expected results.

This is a different kind of representation crisis that is often forgotten because, although there is an apparent representational process and procedures (elections and parliamentary proceedings), there is no real, substantive representation. As a consequence, people seek ways to channel their voice outside the formal representational channels. Over the years, this problem has become chronic and functions subversively to erode the trust in political parties, politicians, parliament, and in the democratic system as a whole. Democratic governance requires the presence of substantive and effective representation. Without it, the democratic institutions and procedures become a democratic façade and, sooner rather than later, will lose its legitimacy.[15] The role of the political party becomes crucial.

---

15 Similar phenomena can also be observed in Europe and the United States with the Occupy Movement and the like, which demand "real democracy" because current democracy has lost much of its meaning and, therefore, loses its legitimacy. See the works of Chantal Mouffe (2000).

4. Good Governance Requires Empowered Citizens

Citizen engagement is an important aspect of good governance. Indeed, by definition, good governance assumes that citizens are engaged in government affairs, not only by giving votes during elections but beyond that in policy making and monitoring. This role can only be played if citizens are empowered by sufficient knowledge of the affairs so that they can participate meaningfully.

The Indonesia Democracy Index data indicate that in the absence of sufficient knowledge, citizens' involvement often does not bring results because they cannot articulate their demands in a way that forces government to respond meaningfully. When involvement does not bring results, it breeds contempt. Knowledgeable citizens, on the other hand, will be able to participate in public affairs beyond demonstration and protests. A knowledgeable citizen may participate consultatively or even collaboratively on public policy matters.

5. Trust in Government Shapes the Form of Citizens' Engagement

Trust in government is an important condition for good governance. This is a type of capital that gives a government an extra cushion in dealing with citizens or when making policies that are not popular in the short term. On the other hand, lack of trust in government will raise skeptical responses from the citizens, even when the government programs or policies are actually sound. Hence, different level of trust will raise different forms of involvement. Trusting citizens will be peaceful and amicable in their criticisms and protests toward the government, whereas distrusting citizens will tend to engage in angry and even violent demonstrations.

Indications from the Indonesia Democracy Index data suggest that Indonesians are very involved in public affairs, and their involvement is continuously increasing. However, this involvement seems to be accompanied by a low level of trust in the government's willingness and ability to respond to their demands. The results often are violent demonstrations.

6. Good Governance Requires Civic Virtues on the Part of the Citizens

Given that the essence of good governance is the relation between the state and society and citizens are the anchor of governance affairs, citizens must possess civic virtues.[16] Good governance requires citizens who know their responsibilities as well as they know their rights. In the good governance concept, civic obligations do not stop at participation in the voting booth but continue throughout the year. Citizens not only have to know their rights but also their obligations; citizens must know that they are free, but they also must know how to express that freedom in a

16 See Sandel (1996) and Allen and Regan (1998) for elaborate discussions on civic virtues. In brief, what I mean here is along the lines of Sandel's generic idea of civic republican citizens who must possess a sense of agency, mastery, community, and trust.

legitimate and democratic manner.

I would argue that the prevalence of demonstrations that end in violence in Indonesia is, to some degree, also a testimony of a condition where civic virtues are low. The combination of a representational crisis, low-performing democratic institutions, ineffective government, and low civic virtues gives rise to the many violent demonstrations that occur throughout Indonesia, from the capital city to villages in remote districts.

References

Agnafors, Marcus. 2013. "Quality of Government: Toward a More Complex Definition." *American Political Science Review* 107 (3): 433–45.

Allen, Anita L., and Milton L. Regan. 1998. *Debating Democracy's Discontent: Essays on American Politics, Law, and Public Philosophy.* Oxford, UK: Oxford University Press.

Bollen, Kenneth A. 1993. "Political Democracy: Conceptual and Measurement Traps." In *On Measuring Democracy*, edited by Alex Inkeles. Brunswick, NJ: Transaction Publisher.

Berggruen, Nicolas, and Nathan Gardels. 2013. *Intelligent Governance for the 21st Century*. Cambridge, UK: Polity Press.

Carothers, Thomas. 2010. "The Illusive Synthesis." *Journal of Democracy* 21 (4): 12–26.

Dahl, Robert. 1971. *Poliarchy: Participation and Opposition.* New Haven, CT: Yale University Press.

Dawood, Yasmin. 2013. "Democracy and the Problem of Partisan State." *Nomos* 54 (Loyalty): 257–91.

Eckardt, Sebastian, and Anwar Shah. 2006. "Local Government Organization and Finance: Indonesia." In *Local Governance in Developing Countries*, edited by Anwar Shah, 233–74. Washington, DC: The World Bank.

Gismar, Abdul Malik. 2011. "After the Big Bang: Governance in Indonesia Democratic Transition." *Jurnal Ekonomi Pembangunan Politik* 7 (2).

Gismar, Abdul Malik. 2010. "Kewarganegaraan dan Kebangsaan." In

Half-Baked Reform, edited by Abdul Malik Gismar and Syarif Hidayat. Jakarta: Teraju.

Grindle, Merilee S. 2010. "Good Governance: The Inflation of an Idea." HKS Faculty Research Working Paper Series, RWP10-023. Cambridge, MA: Harvard University, John F. Kennedy School of Government.

Grindle, Merilee S. 2004. "Good Enough Governance: Poverty Reduction and Reform in Developing Countries." *Governance* 17 (4): 525–48.

Hidayat, Syarif. 2007. *Too Much Too Soon: Local State Elite's Perspective on and the Puzzle of Contemporary Indonesian Regional Autonomy Policy*. Jakarta: Rajawali Press.

Hyden, Goran. 2012. *African Politics in Comparative Perspective*, 2nd ed. Cambridge, UK: Cambridge University Press.

Indeks Demokrasi Indonesia 2014. Ketimpangan antara Institusi dan Kultur Demokrasi. January 29, 2016. http://www.idiproject.org/index.php/en/component/content/article/40-reports/178-indeks-demokrasi-indonesia-2014.

Lifton, Robert Jay. 1993. *The Protean Self: Human Resilience in the Age of Fragmentation.* New York: Basic Books.

Mouffe, Chantal. 2000. *The Democratic Paradox.* London: Verso.

Rothstein, Bo. 2011. *The Quality of Government.* Chicago: University of Chicago Press.

Rustow, Dankwart. 1970. "Transitions to Democracy: Toward a Dynamic Model." In *Transitions to Democracy*, edited by Lisa Anderson, 14–41. New York: Columbia University Press.

Sandel, Michael. 1996. *Democracy and Its Discontent: America in Search of Public Philosophy.* Cambridge, MA: Harvard

University Press.

Tiihonen, Seppo. 2004. *From Governing to Governance: A Process of Change.* Tampere, Finland: Tampere University Press.

Part 2

Good Government in Northeast Asia

5

Policy Representation in Japan: A Longitudinal Study

Willy Jou
Waseda University, Japan

Introduction

Many studies on governance utilize the theoretical concepts on components of 'good governance' developed by the World Bank (e.g. Weiss 2000), as well as empirical data provided by the Worldwide Governance Indicators (WGI). These measures comprise six categories: voice and accountability; political stability and absence of violence; government effectiveness; regulatory quality; the rule of law; and control of corruption. While government performance in all of the above dimensions can affect individual lives, most ordinary citizens could only exert an influence on the first set of indicators, which includes 'perceptions of the extent to which a country's citizens are able to participate in selecting their government.' There is a long scholarly tradition addressing this theme of representation, and this chapter attempts to build on concepts and findings from the extant literature to discuss a key question with respect to political accountability in Japan: to what extent do election results reflect the preferences of the governed?

On the premise that electoral representation often operates through political parties, numerous works have been devoted to exploring relationships between parties and voters. Whereas the early literature often portrays party-voter ties through socio-demographic cleavage structures, particularly economic status (most famously in Lipset and Rokkan 1967), more recent works point to a decline in the explanatory power of class as a predictor of party choice and a concomitant rise in issue-based voting behavior (Clark et al. 2001; Franklin et al. 1992). This trend shifts the central question in political representation from ascriptive to policy representation, namely the correspondence in issue preferences between party-based governments and voters. The degree to which voters' collective views are reflected by parties and governments has attracted considerable scholarly attention (Barnes 1977; Converse and Pierce 1986; Dalton 1985; Hill and Hurley 1999; Huber and Powell 1994; McAllister 1991; Powell 2004), since a fundamental component of political accountability lies in the alignment of elite opinion with the mass public. According to Page and Shapiro, "the responsiveness of government policy to citizens' preferences is a central concern in normative democratic theory" (1983, 175).

Many of these works rely on comparisons between separately conducted elite and mass surveys, but this approach raises doubts that party positions identified by each group are "not conceptually analogous", i.e. ordinary citizens and elites do not necessarily perceive either the contours of policy spaces or parties' stances on various issues through a similar lens. In addition, for any given party, the range of its supporters' views usually exceeds those of its leaders, thus reflecting different distributions (Pierce 1999, 14). In investigating the extent of accountability of the governors to the governed, I circumvent these concerns by taking advantages of recent cross-national surveys which contain information on voter perceptions of party locations in the policy space. This permits an update on the quality of representation by examining the proximity (or otherwise) between governments and voters in Japan during a period of considerable party system changes.

This chapter takes up Powell and Vanberg's call for conducting "analysis of left-right congruence... between the citizen median and the positions of parliamentary governments" (2000, 411), and is organized as follows: The next section offers a selective review of the extensive literature on theories of responsible party government and the policy-centered nature of party competition and cabinet formation, followed by a brief discussion on the utility of the left-right dimension as a device for encapsulating policies and its applicability to new democracies. Section three provides background information about party system changes and issue dimensions that shape policy competition in Japan. Section four introduces hypotheses and data, and section five presents empirical findings on the congruence between government positions and collective public opinion from a longitudinal perspective. The final section discusses both the positive and negative conclusions regarding representation and accountability in Japan.

Programmatic Basis of Responsible Party Government

In a majority of parliamentary systems even candidates who claim an individual, territorially based mandate can rarely exert any influence on policy-making except through their affiliation with parties. In most cases, party labels matter more than personal credentials in determining election results. Party nomination is naturally even more crucial for candidates elected through proportional lists. Consequently, while some studies explore agreement or otherwise between individual legislators and their constituents (Miller and Stokes 1963; Shapiro et al. 1990), it is the degree of congruence between parties and voters that carries greater implications for the quality of policy representation, and a party's positions usually match those of its supporters (Converse and Pierce 1986; Iversen 1994; Przeworski et al. 1999). Individual representatives can modify their views to accord more closely with their constituents (Elling 1982). Do governments respond to public sentiments in a similar manner, or else risk being replaced by competitors who stand closer to the average voter?

The proposition of responsible party government (e.g. Adams 2001; Blondel and Cotta 2001; Castles and Wildenmann 1986) rests on three fundamental conditions: first, parties present different policy alternatives; second, voters choose parties which are closest to their own policy preferences; and third, parties possess the cohesion and discipline to enact their policy promises if they acquire power (Thomassen 1994, 251-252).[17] On the latter requirement, Bowler et al. (1999), Owens (2003), and Sieberer (2006) all highlight the importance of parties acting in a unified manner when voting on legislative proposals. While enforced through reward and censure mechanisms, party cohesion and discipline often derive more fundamentally from shared policy objectives among legislators based on which parties appeal to the electorate. Consequently, a central principle in the responsible party government thesis implies that failure to adhere to these conditions, either in the form of deviation from publicly stated policy goals or disunity among party representatives, invites *collective* sanction, i.e. that voters mete out punishment to parties as a whole rather than individual leaders or legislators.

Policy Cohesion in Coalition Governments

While single-party governments are certainly not immune to internal disunity or reneging on their platforms, it is in cases of multi-party governments where these potential problems are compounded by the need for concessions to coalition partners. Parties can most directly influence policy outcomes through participation in government, yet entering coalitions almost invariably require compromising policy goals. The balance between

17 One can also include the specific criterion that voters must possess both clear preferences and sufficient knowledge to distinguish among party programs.

policy- and office-seeking objectives has long preoccupied works on coalition theory (e.g. Budge and Laver 1993; Laver and Budge 1992; Schofeld 1993), but several studies affirm that programmatic objectives predominate. For example, Bagdanor (1983) asserts that commitment to policies "carry an overriding weight" for parties, and Hofferbert and Klingemann (1990) show that parties utilize office as a means of attaining policy goals, rather than vice versa. Furthermore, Klingemann et al. (1994) show that parties do indeed turn platform promises into policies when they enter into government, though in cases of multi-party governments this linkage may be complicated by cabinet portfolio allocation and contents of coalition agreements. It is also important to keep in mind that the same policy outcome may prove beneficial to one coalition partner but detrimental to another, depending on the different programmatic goals each espouses, because "voters compare coalition parties to one another and judge performance with regard to what the parties stand for" (Anderson 1995, 379).[18]

Also relevant for the purpose of this study are findings on the linkage between positions of each coalition government and its participating parties (for a review see Warwick 2001). Some scholars focus on the preponderant roles of parties providing the prime minister, the finance minister, or the coalition formateur, but since cabinet portfolio allocation is generally proportional to participating

18 For example, Powell and Whitten's (1993) finding that policies favoring the public sector and private enterprises reap electoral rewards for left- and right-wing parties, respectively, demonstrate that the criteria for voters' assessment lie in each party's adherence to its issue priorities.

parties' parliamentary strength, with the largest party nominating the prime minister, one can assume that controlling for relative party size within a coalition government addresses the effect of differential influence each portfolio carries.

The theory of responsible party government also rests on the assumptions that parties participating in coalitions not only care about policies, but also exercise control, or at least exert major impact, over decision making. Budge and Keman affirmed this proposition, stating that it is valid to regard parties as "a) being concerned with policy, since they exert a consistent and important influence over it; b) being important decision-makers and actors, since they move policies in the direction of their own preferences and values" (1990, 158). Extending this argument, parties may pursue policies in line with their ideological orientations even when these do not bring immediate electoral benefits, since doing so reinforces their identity and credibility. In sum, we can assume that parties in government exercise significant control over the direction of policies, and that the overall policy positions of a coalition government approximate the average stances of participating parties, controlling for their relative weight within the coalition.[19] In the case of single-party government, there should be a more direct relationship between cabinet composition and policy outcome.

---

19 In addition to its number of parliamentary seats, a party's weight may also be affected by whether it is a pivotal coalition member, i.e. if the government can survive without its support.

Measuring Voter-Government Distance

To capture both voters' and governments' policy positions and assess the propinquity between these two measures, it is necessary to operationalize policy distance. Most previous studies utilize a generic left-right dimension as a useful means of summarizing stances in a wide array of issue areas. These spatial labels have long been used as a means of summarizing and communicating political information (Fuchs and Klingemann 1989; Mair 2007), because they serve as convenient heuristics that link diverse and sometimes disconnected policy dimensions, and thus simplifies political choices for voters lacking detailed knowledge of where parties stand on various issues (Conover and Feldman 1984; Sniderman et al. 1993). While one does not frequently find political competition in any country consistently evolving solely around a single axis, heuristics encapsulate the most salient issues of the day, and can serve as a "universal solvent" sufficiently flexible to absorb new issues when they become salient (Barnes 1997, 131). Since "the left-right dimension is more often than not used by political elites and mass communication to label the most important issues of a given era" (Inglehart and Klingemann 1976:244), and explains substantial variance in voting behavior in many established democracies (Knutsen 1995; Van der Eijk et al. 2005), we follow previous practice in using this schema to gauge proximity between voters and governments.

As evidence that ideological congruence shape voter-party linkages, studies have shown that in established democracies, a party's voters and elites share similarities in both positions along the left-right spectrum and preferences on specific issues (Holmberg 2000; Schmitt and Thomassen 1999). These conclusions lend further support to theories of responsible party government, in the sense that voters choose a party on the basis of policy agreement, and are likely to decide whether to continue supporting this party by assessing its willingness and ability to carry out its programmatic promises if it enters government. This places a constraint on parties, and therefore governments, which may be tempted to seek radical departures from the platforms they present to voters at election time. However, the match between the views of a party's leaders and supporters varies across policies areas. Instead of examining specific issues, we follow Huber and Powell (1994, 293) in using the left-right dimension as a common benchmark for measuring voter-elite congruence, since studies have shown a stronger voter-party correspondence in left-right terms than on individual policies such as employment and border control (Thomassen and Schmitt 1997, 177-180).

Party Competition and Voting Behavior in Japan

While left-right semantics originated in Western Europe, studies have shown that citizens in other parts of the world are able to understand and align themselves along this ideological scale (e.g. Dalton 2006; McAllister and White 2007). It is crucial to keep in mind that this does not necessarily imply that the same policy dimensions structure left-right orientations everywhere.[20] In contrast to class cleavage dominant in many Western European countries, economic issues have traditionally played a minor role in Japanese party competition, because "both progressive and conservative political parties have endorsed expanded welfare services," and shared a consensus concerning government intervention in the economy (Otake 2000, 128). This also holds true at the individual level, evidenced for instance in a 2004 survey showing that respondents identifying with different parties held similar positions on welfare issues (Hirano 2005, 74-75). Another study reports that individual self-placements on the ideological scale are not significantly correlated with their views on either income inequality or welfare (Ida 2007, 182-83).

Instead, analysis of both party documents and expert surveys finds that foreign and defense policies exert a large influence on party locations on the ideological scale (Laver and Benoit 2005; Proksch et al. 2011).[21] During the Cold War, debates over foreign and security policies pitted defenders of the US-drafted "pacifist" constitution against advocates of constitutional revision aimed at allowing Japan to maintain a full-fledged army and play a more

20 Powell and Vanberg observe that using the left-right dimension as an analytical tool does not require these spatial labels to carry the same meanings (2000, 385).

21 Furthermore, this dimension might include attitudes toward the very nature of the postwar Japanese polity, as voters at the progressive end of the spectrum were much more likely to harbor anti-system sentiments (Tanaka 1995).

active role in regional security. Indeed, "the defense issue emerged in the early 1950s, and the pattern of conservative-progressive confrontation was institutionalized by the 1960 political crisis over the renewal of the [US-Japan] Security Treaty, shaping Japanese politics for the next 30 years" (Otake 2000, 128). This axis of political competition is found not only among elites, but also at the level of ordinary citizens. Kohei et al.'s (1991) examination of voter surveys show that, out of four issue clusters, party choice was robustly correlated only with the one pertaining to security questions. Given that "policy based party competition in Japan is inherently one dimensional" (Laver and Benoit 2005, 202), it is not surprising that Japanese voters are able to both identify parties along a uni-dimensional ideological spectrum and rank them consistently (Kabashima and Takenaka 1996).

Party System Changes

As the Cold War came to an end in the early 1990s, the Japanese party system entered a state of flux, involving the split of the long-ruling Liberal Democratic Party (LDP) and the establishments, mergers, and splits of new parties, such as the New Frontier Party (NFP) and the Democratic Party of Japan (DPJ). The formation of a coalition government between the LDP and the Japan Socialist Party (JSP), which had sharply opposed one another for nearly four decades, seemed to signal the declining relevance of ideology in politics. However, this does not mean that all ideological divisions have disappeared. In the eyes of both academic and media observers, the LDP on the one hand, and the Japanese Communist Party (JDP) and Social Democratic Party (SDP; successor to the JSP) on the other, continue to anchor the conservative and progressive ends of the spectrum, respectively. The latter two parties, however, have relatively minor parliamentary presence. Instead, the DPJ, located around the ideological center ground but encompassing disparate policy views, emerged as the main competitor to the LDP during the 2000s, and formed the government during 2009-2012.[22]

Several studies have affirmed that ideological orientations do indeed have a significant effect on vote choice in Japan (Miyake 1988; Kabashima and Takenana 1996). However, party system changes have contributed to the weakening of this influence by the early 2000s. According to Kabashima and Takenaka (2012), ideology still exerts an impact when voters choose between the LDP and the long-established but now minor leftist parties, the SDP and JCP, but not when it comes to the choice between the two major parties, the LDP and DPJ. This is mainly attributable to the latter party's less clearly defined ideological profile.

Inglehart and Klingemann stated in their seminal study that, in times of major party system transformation, left-right orientations can "provide an important cue in channeling voters from their former party to the nearest equivalent among the new ones" (1976, 271). This means that ideological labels may perform a more important heuristic role precisely when voters are faced with an

22 The DPJ merged with another party to form the Democratic Party (DP) at the end of March 2016.

array of new and unfamiliar choices on the ballot and cannot rely on long-held party identification as cues, as has been the case in Japan since in the past quarter-century. Also, one should note that coalition governments have become the norm since the 1990s.[23] Even when a single party holds a majority of seats in the House of Representatives (lower chamber), it usually chooses to form a coalition with one or more small parties to secure a majority in the House of Councillors (upper chamber), and also for purposes of campaign coordination. Coalition preferences are always indicated in advance of elections, so voters supporting a given party are aware of which coalition partners it would have if it enters government.

Hypotheses and Data

If governments accurately reflect collective public choice, we expect a match between policy positions of governments and electorates across time. I test whether the following hypotheses hold true: 1) election results, as measured by vote shares garnered by each party, reflect aggregate voter preferences; 2) right-(left-)leaning

23 Coalition governments since the early 1990s are: 7-party non-LDP coalition (including JSP and Komeito, 1993-4); 5-party non-LDP coalition (including Komeito, 1994); LDP-JSP-Sakigake coalition (1994-6); LDP-Liberal Party coalition (1999); LDP-Komeito-Liberal Party coalition (1999-2000); LDP-Komeito-Conservative Party coalition (2000-3); LDP-Komeito coalition (2003-9, 2012-present); DPJ-SDP-People's New Party coalition (2009-10); DPJ-People's New Party coalition (2010-12).

electorates correspond to right-(left-)leaning governments, either through adjustment by incumbents or changes of cabinet. Based on previous studies which find that more parties are located nearer either pole of the left-right spectrum than their respective supporters, we infer that the average left-right position of the overall electorate is likely to be relatively centrist, compared with governments comprised of parties identified with one end of the ideological scale or the other. A shift in collective public opinion that leads to executive replacement is therefore likely to see the government position along the left-right scale swing much more sharply than the change in average voter position.[24]

A number of waves in the Japan Election Study (JES) survey series are used for the purpose of investigating voter-government congruence, since respondents are asked to give not only self-placements, but also to identify the positions of major parties, on the same ideological scale. Specifically, JES data are available for the 1983, 1995, 2004 and 2007 House of Councillors (upper chamber) elections. For more recent years, I utilize a survey by a research tem at Waseda University for the 2010 upper chamber elections, and two on-line surveys conducted at the time of the 2012 and 2014 House of Representatives (lower chamber) elections.[25] While elections to

---

24 In this chapter, the terms 'conservative' and 'progressive' are used interchangeably with 'right' and 'left', respectively. The former set of terms have long been more widely used in Japan than the latter.

25 Datasets are made available by SSJDA at the University of Tokyo, the Center of Institutional Construction at Waseda University, and Leviathan Databank. JES I was conducted in June and December 1983; JES II, between 1993-1996; JES

the two chambers utilize different mechanisms to translate votes into seats, I focus on respondents' evaluations of self and party ideological positions, which should not be affected by these different institutional rules. Thus, for the purpose of this chapter, surveys for upper and lower chamber elections are comparable.

One can argue that some voters may lack sufficient political sophistication to accurately identify where parties stand, so that their responses could be either random, or biased by persuasion and projection effects through which voters locate preferred parties close to their own positions to justify their vote choice. Without ruling out such possibility, there is reason to believe that individual biases are likely to cancel out one another. Furthermore, even when subjective responses deviate from parties' "objective" stances, one must remember that voters are much more likely to decide how to mark their ballots based on the former criterion. Finally, the absence of expert surveys for some of the elections covered in this study means that no alternative measure of party positions is available.

Voter and Party Positions

The mean placements for all parties included in each survey are shown in table 1. Some of the earlier surveys did not solicit

III, between 2001-2005; JES IV, between 2007-2011. The other surveys were conducted at the time of each specific election.

respondents' opinion on minor parties, but for each election the total vote share of parties listed in the table exceeds 90 percent. Parties belonging to the incumbent governing coalition at the time of each election are underlined. All placements are standardized based on a 0-10 scale, with higher values denoting a more conservative stance. The fact that only the Liberal Democratic Party (LDP) and Japanese Communist Party (JCP) are included in questionnaires throughout the period covered by this study testify to extensive fluctuations in the party system described in the preceding section.

Respondents have consistently rated the LDP as the most conservative party, while the JCP has, with one single exception (in 2012), retained the same reputation on the progressive end of the scale. That said, if one traces changes in the perceived ideological positions of these two parties, one would easily observe centripetal trends (a reversal in 2014 notwithstanding). The magnitude of the shift is greater on the left than on the right. As a consequence, the party system today is less polarized than three decades ago. Also worth noting is the impact of joining a governing coalition on smaller parties: the traditionally leftist Japan Socialist Party (JSP) was seen to have shifted dramatically toward the center in 1995, when it joined a coalition dominated by the LDP; Komeito, a religiously based party commonly regarded as centrist during the 1970s and 1980s, has come to be perceived as a conservative force since joining a LDP-led coalition in the late 1990s.

Table 1. **Perceived party positions**

	1983	1995	2004	2007	2010	2012	2014
LDP	8.1	7.34	7.3	7.3	6.7	7	7.63
JCP	1.55	2.92	2.83	3.11	4.09	4.54	3.75
JSP/SDP	2.95	5.04	3.92	4.14	4.68	4.99	
Komeito	5.28		6.12	6.46	5.77	6.34	7.01
DSP	3.44						
NFP		5.86					
Sakigake		5.38					
DPJ			5.3	5.09	5.1	5.67	5.55
NRP					5.04	5.03	
YP					4.72	4.67	
PNP					5.45	5.73	
JRP						3.84	4.67
Tomorrow						4.72	
PFG							6.59

LDP = Liberal Democratic Party; JCP = Japanese Communist Party; JSP/SDP = Japan Socialist Party/Social Democratic Party (name change in 1996); DSP = Democratic Socialist Party; NFP = New Frontier Party; DPJ = Democratic Party of Japan; NRP = New Renaissance Party; YP = Your Party; PNP = People's New Party; JRP = Japan Restoration Party; Tomorrow = Tomorrow Party of Japan; PFG = Party for Future Generations

The mean respondent positions at the time of all elections for which data are available are given in table 2. Note that while questions on ideological self-placement are included in most surveys, respondents are not always asked to place parties on the same scale, so there are more time points shown here than in table 1. Not surprisingly – and similar to most other established democracies – the Japanese public has remained relatively centrist over time, with the mean usually close to the midpoint (5.0) of the ideological scale. At the same time, one can see that the electorate has consistently veered slightly toward the right, as the mean value never once registered below 5.0. Interestingly, table 2 suggests that when the conservative LDP suffered setback at the polls, such as in the 2007 House of Councillors and 2009 House of Representatives elections, it was *not* due to a general progressive shift among the public. Indeed the DPJ, the biggest winner in those elections and the most viable alternative to the LDP as a governing party, had never been perceived as a center-left party throughout its history.

Table 2. Mean ideological position of the general public

survey year	position	data source
1983	5.4	JES I
1993	5.33	JES II
1995	5.01	JES II
2003	5.43	JES III
2004	5.4	JES III
2005	5.46	JES III
2007	5.52	JES IV
2009	5.33	JES IV
2010	5.28	Waseda-CASI 2010
2012	5.13	web survey
2014	5.38	web survey

Note: Mean placement on ideological scale; standardized on 0-10 scale (0 = most progressive; 10 = most conservative)
JES = Japan Election Study

At a first glance, one may thus conclude that the accountability mechanism functions well in Japan: a center-right electorate has always been represented by center-right governments (see left column of table 3 below). Indeed, while no comparable public opinion surveys were conducted in the first few decades following

World War II, many scholars would not doubt that this correspondence between the majority of voters and their government on the conservative side of the ideological spectrum also applied during those years. The question of whether center-left parties could gain the reins of power following a leftward swing in the public mood has so far remained moot, and one has little reason to expect that an occasion to test this proposition would arise in the foreseeable future.

Do Election Results Reflect the Popular Will?

We are interested in whether the results of each election resembled the aggregate (self-expressed) preference of the public more than the incumbent government did. *Election result* is calculated by the position of each party for which we have data, weighed by vote shares.[26] For example, if a centrist electorate is located at 5.0, and a right-wing incumbent government at 7.0, we expect the *election result* to fall somewhere between these two points. Furthermore, one can consider an *election result* registering below 6.0 to be a more accurate reflection of the popular will than a result above this figure. Technically there is nothing to inhibit a left-

26 I use vote rather than seat shares to avoid problems produced by disproportionality, as both chambers of the Japanese legislature are elected by parallel mixed systems rather than proportional representation (PR). Vote shares refer to each party's performance in the party list, not district, tier.

wing party from garnering such a high vote share that the election would yield a result below 5.0, realistically such scenario had long been – and still remains – improbable.

The position of incumbent governments, calculated by taking account of the vote shares of each coalition partner in the preceding House of Representatives election (only lower chamber election results determine cabinet formation), are shown in the left column of table 3. Note that the incumbent government is not necessarily the same as the cabinet which took office following the preceding lower chamber election, as was the case in 1995 (i.e. there were changes in cabinet composition during the legislative period).

The right column of table 3 replicates data in table 2 for those years when survey respondents were asked to give both self and party ideological placements. *Election results* are shown in the center column. In line with expectations, at every point in time, *election results* fall between the positions of the aggregate electorate and the incumbent government. To put it another way, one can think of these outcomes as an expression of voters' collective wish for the government to shift its policies closer to their own preferences. This was particularly striking in 1983 and 2007: *election results* were much nearer the electorate's ideal point than that of the government, meaning that voters delivered rebuke to cabinets seen as veering too far toward the right. The 2004 election yielded a similar, if less dramatic, outcome, and this result was also widely reported as a defeat for the incumbent coalition. Since these were elections for the upper chamber, governments were not required to resign after losing so long as they still commanded a majority in the lower chamber. Nevertheless, one can consider these examples of accountability, of the public clearly indicating its disapproval of the direction of government policies.

Table 3. **Government positions, election results, public position**

	government position	incumbent government	election result	public position
1983	8.10	LDP	5.70	5.40
1995	6.60	LDP-JSP-Sakigake	5.82	5.01
2004	6.95	LDP-Komeito	5.78	5.40
2007	7.03	LDP-Komeito	5.75	5.52
2010	5.67	DPJ-PNP	5.46	5.28
2012	5.67	DPJ-PNP	5.51	5.13
2014	6.80	LDP-Komeito	6.15	5.38

Note: *government position* calculated by position of each governing party weighed by vote share; *election result* calculated by position of each party weighed by its vote share in the proportional tier of the election

By contrast, one has reason to question the accountability mechanism when looking at results for the 2012 and 2014 polls -- a question that is all the more important because these are lower chamber elections that determine cabinet composition. In 2012, voters turned their back to a perceived center-right government, yet the apparently centrist election result concealed significant gains for two parties placed at the most conservative and most progressive ends of the spectrum (the LDP and Japan Restoration Party, respectively). Furthermore, the election led to a right-wing coalition (LDP-Komeito) coming to power, one that is further away from the ideal point of the electorate than its predecessor. The 2014 result, at 6.15, is further to the right than at any time in the past three decades, despite the public remaining relatively centrist. Instead of opting in greater numbers for parties (perceived to be) espousing centrist or progressive views, a centrist electorate awarded a right-wing coalition with another overwhelming legislative majority. This apparent paradox raises doubts about the quality of representation, and thus the quality of governance, in Japan today.

Summary and Conclusion

The preceding pages have investigated the question of how accurately citizen preferences in Japan are reflected by elections, the most common channel through which the public holds their government accountable. While previous approaches to this important topic mostly relied on separate surveys of voters and party elites (or country experts), this chapter has taken advantage of public opinion surveys that ask respondents to place both themselves and major parties on the same ideological scale. Results show that the collective inclination of a centre -right electorate has always corresponded with center-right cabinets; furthermore, election results have consistently fallen between the positions of the public and the incumbent government on a spatial spectrum that summarizes major issues. This suggests that elections indeed serve as instruments of democracy (Powell 2000), partly by means of voters sanctioning governments that pursue policies at variance with their collective preferences.

While this seems to be encouraging news regarding the accountability dimension of governance in Japan, another finding sounds alarm bells. As explained earlier in the chapter, cabinets often occupy a more extreme location toward either end of the ideological spectrum than the mean position of the public, so the fact that all governments covered by the present study is situated further to the right than the electorate does not by itself diminish the quality of representation. Rather, one cause for concern lies in the wide gap between the electorate's ideal point and the outcome of the most recent election (in 2014) in terms of parties' vote shares: public opinion has shifted little from its usual moderate stance, but the election result emerges further to the right than ever before. Just as worrying for those who profess faith in accountability through the ballot box is the fact that while voters indicated a preference for a centripetal shift in the 2012 polls, the election actually led to the formation of a cabinet more conservative than its predecessor. This is partly due to how the electoral system translates votes into legislative seats, which is an institutional feature with limited prospects of rectification. However, another likely cause – one more pertinent to the question of accountability – is fragmentation among opposition parties. Without a credible alternative that threatens to replace it, the government has less need to worry about potential chastisement at the ballot box, and may therefore feel fewer constraints with respect to being accountable to the public.

In view of the findings reported above, it is worthwhile to return to the long-debated question regarding the direction of policy influence. Jacobs and Shapiro point to considerable evidence from previous research that public opinion prompts elite responses in virtually a one-way relationship (1994:12), and Kuklinski and Segura also stress a predominant emphasis among empirical research on representation that citizens' views are exogenous to policy-making (1995,17-18). In contrast, Holmberg places numerical weights on the relative importance of elite-driven (65%) and public-driven (35%) issue congruence (1997, 280). Since this chapter does not utilize elite data, it is not possible to trace changes and continuities in policy-makers' views. Also, the survey data used here do not allow one to examine whether and how much a government actually changes course in response to shifts in public opinion during its term of office. In other words, how to ensure the accountability of the governors to the governed not only at the ballot box, but also between one election and the next? These questions of elite opinion and mid-term accountability are topics worth exploring in future studies.

References

Adams, James (2001). *Party Competition and Responsible Party Government: A Theory of Spatial Competition Based upon Insights from Behavioral Voting Research.* Ann Arbor: University of Michigan Press.

Anderson, Christopher J. 1995. 'The Dynamics of Public Support for Coalition Governments.' *Comparative Political Studies* 28(3): 350-83.

Bagdanor, Vernon. 1983. *Coalition Government in Western Europe.* London: Heinemann.

Barnes, Samuel H. 1977. *Representation in Italy: Institutionalized Tradition and Electoral Choice.* Chicago: University of Chicago Press.

Barnes, Samuel H. 1997. 'Electoral Behavior and Comparative Politics.' In *Comparative Politics: Rationality, Culture, and Structure*, eds. Mark Irving Lichback and Alan S. Zuckerman. Cambridge: Cambridge University Press.

Blondel, Jean, and Maurizio Cotta (eds.). 2000. *The Nature of Party Government: A Comparative European Perspective.* New York: Palgrave.

Bowler, Shaun, David M. Farrell, and Richard S. Katz. 1999. *Party Discipline and Parliamentary Government.* Columbus: Ohio State University Press.

Budge, Ian, and Hans Keman. 1990. *Parties and Democracy: Coalition Formation and Government Functioning in Twenty States.* Oxford: Oxford University Press.

Budge, Ian, and Michael Laver. 1993. 'The Policy Basis of Government Coalitions: A Comparative Investigation.' *British Journal of Political Science* 23: 499-519.

Castles, Francis G., and Rudolf Wildenmann (eds.) 1986. *Visions and Realities of Party Government*. Berlin: Walter de Gruyter.

Clark, Terry Nichols, Seymour Martin Lipset, and Michael Rempel (2001). 'The Declining Political Significance of Social Class.' In *The Breakdown of Class Politics: A Debate of Post-Industrial Stratification*, eds. Terry Nichols Clark and Seymour Martin Lipset. Baltimore: Johns Hopkins University Press.

Conover, Pamela Johnston, and Stanley Feldman. 1984. 'How People Organize the Political World: A Schematic Model.' *American Journal of Political Science* 28(1): 95-126.

Converse, Philip E., and Roy Pierce. 1986. *Political Representation in France*. Cambridge: Belknap Press of Harvard University Press.

Dalton, Russell J. 1985. 'Political Parties and Political Representation.' *Comparative Political Studies* 18(3): 267-99.

Dalton, Russell J. 2006. 'Social Modernization and the End of Ideology Debate: Patterns of Ideological Polarization.' *Japanese Journal of Political Science* 7: 1-22.

Elling, Richard C. 1982. 'Ideological Change in the U.S. Senate: Time and Electoral Responsiveness.' *Legislative Studies Quarterly* 7(1): 75-92.

Franklin, Mark N., Thomas T. Mackie, and Henry Valen (eds.). 1992. *Electoral Change: Responses to Evolving Social and Attitudinal Structures in Western Countries*. Cambridge: Cambridge University Press.

Fuchs, Dieter, and Hans-Dieter Klingemann. 1989. 'The Left-Right

Schema.' In *Continuities in Political Action: A Longitudinal Study of Political Orientations in Three Western Democracies*, M. Kent Jennings, Jan W. van Deth et al. Berlin: Walter de Gruyter.

Hill, Kim Quaile, and Patricia A. Hurley. 1999. 'Dyadic Representation Reappraised.' *American Journal of Political Science* 43(1): 109-37.

Hirano, Hiroshi. 2007. *Henyo-suru Nihon no Shakai no Tohyo kodo*. Tokyo: Bokutakusha.

Hofferbert, Richard I., and Hans-Dieter Klingemann. 1990. 'The Policy Impact of Party Programmes and Government Declarations in the Federal Republic of Germany.' *European Journal of Political Research* 18(3): 277-304.

Holler 1982

Holmberg, Sören. 1997. 'Dynamic Opinion Representation.' *Scandinavian Political Studies* 20(3): 265-83.

Holmberg, Sören. 2000. 'Issue Agreement.' In *Beyond Westminster and Congress: The Nordic Experience*, eds. Peter Esaiasson and Knut Heidar. Columbus: Ohio State University Press.

Huber, John D., and G. Bingham Powell. 1994. 'Congruence between Citizens and Policymakers in Two Visions of Liberal Democracy.' *World Politics* 46(3): 291-326.

Ida, Masamichi. 2007. *Nihon Seiji no Choryu: Daitoryousei-ka, Nidai-seito-ka, Datsu Seito*. Tokyo: Hokuju Shuppan.

Inglehart, Ronald, and Hans Klingemann. 1976. 'Party Identification, Ideological Preference and the Left-Right Dimension among Western Mass Publics.' In *Party Identification and Beyond*, eds. Ian Budge, Ivor Crewe, and Dennis Farlie. London: Wiley.

Iversen, Torben. 1994. 'Political Leadership and Representation in West European Democracies: A Test of Three Models of Voting.' *American Journal of Political Science* 38(1): 45-74.

Jacobs, Lawrence R., and Robert Y. Shapiro. 1994. 'Studying Substantive Democracy.' *PS: Political Science and Politics* 27(1): 9-17.

Kabashima, Ikuo, and Yoshikiho Takenaka. 1996. *Gendai Nihonjin no Ideorogii*. Tokyo: University of Tokyo Press.

Kabashima, Ikuo, and Yoshihiko Takenaka. 2012. *Ideorogii*. Tokyo: University of Tokyo Press.

Klingemann, Hans-Dieter, Richard I. Hofferbert, and Ian Budge. 1994. *Parties, Policies, and Democracy*. Boulder: Westview.

Knutsen, Oddbjørn. 1995. 'Party Choice.' In *The Impact of Values*, eds. Jan W. van Deth and Elinor Scarbrough. Oxford: Oxford University Press.

Kohei, Shinsaku, Ichiro Miyake, and Joji Watanuki. 1991. Issues and Voting Behavior. In *The Japanese Voter*, eds. Scott C. Flanagan, Shinsaku Kohei, Ichiro Miyake, Bradley M. Richardson, and Joji Watanuki. New Haven: Yale University Press.

Kuklilnski, James H., and Gary M. Segura. 1995. 'Endogeneity, Exogeneity, Time, and Space in Political Representation.' *Legislative Studies Quarterly* 20(1): 3-21.

Laver, Michael, and Kenneth Benoit. 2005. 'Estimating Party Policy Positions: Japan in Comparative Context.' *Japanese Journal of Political Science* 6(2): 187-209.

Laver, Michael, and Ian Budge. 1992. *Party Policy and Government Coalitions*. New York: St. Martin's Press.

Lipset, Seymour M., and Stein Rokkan. 1967. 'Cleavage Structures,

Party Systems, and Voter Alignments: An Introduction.' In *Party Systems and Voter Alignments: Cross-National Perspectives*, eds. Seymour M. Lipset and Stein Rokkan. New York: Free Press.

Mair, Peter. 2007. 'Left-Right Orientations.' In *The Oxford Handbook of Political Behavior*, eds. Russell J. Dalton and Hans-Dieter Klingemann. Oxford: Oxford University Press.

McAllister, Ian. 1991. 'Party Elites, Voters and Political Attitudes: Testing Three Explanations for Mass-Elite Differences.' *Canadian Journal of Political Science* 24: 237-68.

McAllister, Ian, and Stephen White. 2007. 'Political Parties and Democratic Consolidation in Post-Communist Societies.' *Party Politics* 13(2): 197-216.

Miller, Warren E., and Donald E. Stokes. 1963. 'Constituency Influence in Congress.' *American Political Science Review* 57(1): 45-56.

Miyake, Ichiro. 1988. *Tohyo Kodo*. Tokyo: University of Tokyo Press.

Otake, Hideo. 2000. 'Political Realignment and Policy Conflict.' In *Power Shuffles and Policy Process: Coalition Government in Japan in the 1990s*, ed. Hideo Otake. Tokyo: Japan Center for International Exchange.

Owens, John E. 2003. 'Explaining Party Cohesion and Discipline in Democratic Legislatures: Purposiveness and Contexts.' *Journal of Legislative Studies* 9(4): 12-40.

Page, Benjamin I., and Robert Y. Shapiro. 1983. 'Effects of Public Opinion on Policy.' *American Political Science Review* 77(1): 175-90.

Pierce, Roy. 1999. 'Mass-Elite Issue Linkages and the Responsible Party Model of Representation.' In *Policy Representation in*

Western Democracies , eds. Warren E. Miller, Roy Pierce, Jacques Thomassen, Richard Herrera, Sören Holmberg, Peter Esaissson, and Bernhard Wessels. Oxford: Oxford University Press.

Powell, G. Bingham. 2000. *Elections as Instruments of Democracy: Majoritarian and Proportional Visions*. New Haven: Yale University Press.

Powell, G. Bingham. 2004. 'Political Representation in Comparative Politics.' *Annual Review of Political Science* 7: 273-96.

Powell, G. Bingham, and Georg S. Vanberg. 2000. 'Election Laws, Disproportionality and Median Correspondence: Implications for Two Visions of Democracy.' *British Journal of Political Science* 30(3): 383-411.

Proksch, Sven-Oliver, Jonathan B. Slapin, and Michael F. Thies. 2011. Party System Dynamics in Post-war Japan: A Quantitative Content Analysis of Electoral Pledges. *Electoral Studies* 30(1): 114-24.

Przeworski, Adam, Susan Carol Stokes, Bernard Manin (eds.). 1999. *Democracy, Accountability, and Representation*. Cambridge: Cambridge University Press.

Schmitt, Hermann, and Jacques Thomassen. 1999. *Political Representation and Legitimacy in the European Union*. Oxford: Oxford University Press.

Schofeld, Norman. 1993. 'Political Competition and Multiparty Coalition Governments.' *European Journal of Political Research* 23(1): 1-33.

Shapiro, Catherine R., David W. Brady, Richard A. Brody, and John A. Ferejohn. 1990. 'Linking Constituency Opinion and Senate

Voting Scores: A Hybrid Explanation.' *Legislative Studies Quarterly* 15(4): 599-621.

Sieberer, Ulrich. 2006. 'Party Unity in Parliamentary Democracies: A Comparative Analysis.' *Journal of Legislative Studies* 12(2): 150-78.

Sniderman, Paul M., Richard A. Brody, and Philip Tetlock. 1993. *Reasoning and Choice: Explorations in Political Psychology*. Cambridge: Cambridge University Press.

Tanaka, Aiji. '1995. 55nen Taisei no Hokai to Sistemu sapoto no Keizoku.' *Leviathan* 17: 52-83.

Thomassen, Jacques. 1994. 'Empirical Research into Political Representation: Failing Democracy or Failing Models?' In *Elections at Home and Abroad: Essays in Honor or Warren E. Miller*, eds. M. Kent Jennings and Thomas E. Mann. Ann Arbor: University of Michigan Press.

Thomassen, Jacques, and Hermann Schmitt. 1997. 'Policy Representation.' *European Journal of Political Research* 32(2): 165-84.

Van der Eijk, Cees, Hermann Schmitt, and Tanja Binder. 2005). 'Left-Right Orientations and Party Choice.' In *The European Voter: A Comparative Study of Modern Democracies*, ed. Jacques Thomassen. Oxford: Oxford University Press.

Warwick, Paul V. 2001. 'Coalition Policy in Parliamentary Democracies.' *Comparative Political Studies* 34(10): 1212-36.

Weiss, Thomas. 2000. 'Governance, Good Governance and Global Governance: Conceptual and Actual Challenges.' *Third World Quarterly* 21(5): 795-814

6

Trust and Democracy: A Ripplelike Pattern in China

Lingling Qi
Nanjing University, China

Introduction

Ever since Putnam's groundbreaking research in *Making Democracy Work* (Putnam, Leonard, and Nanetti 1993), the social capital theory has flourished in political science and other social sciences. Social capital, mainly referring to civic engagement and trust (Putnam 1995), is regarded as an indispensable ingredient for the functioning of fine democracy (e.g., Almond and Verba 1963; Cook 2001; Fukuyama 1995; Hardin 2001; Inglehart 1997; Jamal and Nooruddin 2010; Newton 1997, 2001; Putnam 1995; Putnam et al. 1993; Sztompka 1999; Uslaner 2002). The past two decades have witnessed numerous empirical studies on related topics, seeking to explore the complex relationships between social capital and multiple dimensions of democracy. With the accumulation of empirical evidence and conflicting comparative results, scholars have started to reflect on the concept of social capital *per se*. They have carefully reexamined the connotation and structure of trust, theoretically (Maloy 2009) and empirically (Delhey, Newton, and Welzel 2011, 2014; van Hoorn 2014) analyzed the relationship among different types of trust (Newton and Zmerli 2011), and broadly investigated the impact of trust in diverse cultural backgrounds. Among these literatures, research that differentiates between the particular trust bestowed upon members of in-groups and general trust across a society produce rather rich outcomes (e.g., Glanville and Paxton 2007; Mishler and Rose 2005, 1053; Nannestad 2008; Newton 1999, 20–21; Putnam 1995, 172; Robbins 2011, 2012; Uslaner 2002; Warren 1999, 8–12; Whiteley 1999; Yosano and Hayashi 2005). Basically, this line of literature advocates that it is imperative to scrutinize dissimilar impacts and mechanisms of two types of trust in society. General trust is usually found to be most important for social capital in a large-scale, mobile, and socially mixed society (Newton and Zmerli 2011, 170), but societies vary in terms of the radius of general trust (Delhey et al. 2011). The discovery of a varying radius of trust leads to a series of interesting questions for comparative civic culturalists, and there is even more curiosity about the impact of particular trust on democracy. Besides the general conclusions drawn from the quantitative studies, there is also interest in the accurate line between particular trust and general trust in certain countries and, as a consequence, how this is related to democracy.

In this chapter, I investigate the Chinese pattern of trust and explore how the particular Chinese trust pattern is associated with democratic values and political activities. The rationale for the study of social capital theory in China, specifically the issue of particular trust and general trust, is threefold.

First, previous large-N comparative analyses of social capital theory have shown China is an outlying case in terms of the relationship between social capital and the level of democracy (Inglehart 1997, 2005; Seligson 2002, 278). Specifically, China, a country with a troubling development of democracy, enjoys a surprisingly high level of interpersonal trust, which naturally leads to the question of why the social capital theory takes a different form in this country. To my knowledge, this puzzle has not been sufficiently addressed by comparativists on China, despite some general analyses of Chinese social capital (e.g., Cao, Zhao, and Ren 2015; Chen and Lu 2007; Palmer, Perkins, and Xu 2011; Steinhardt 2012; Xu, Perkins, and Chow 2010). Second, the social capital theory has been largely developed in a Western setting, and social capital is found to be closely associated with key societal characteristics. Therefore, it is rather interesting to explore the structure of social capital in an entirely foreign culture. Given the drastic modernization process in present-day China, to what extent do modern factors or the unique Confucian traditions influence Chinese interpersonal trust as well as political activities? Third, the importance of social capital theory in China also stems from China's democratic development. Civic culturalists are persistently interested in the citizens' civic and political attitudes in China's resilient authoritarian regime (Nathan 2003). Comparativists are not only motivated to solve the puzzle of China as an outlier of social capital theory but are also concerned with China's democratization process in general.

Using data collected in the city of Nanjing, China, following the local People's Congress election in 2012, I found persisting differential circles of trust in family members, relatives and friends, schoolmates, acquaintances, colleagues, and strangers in China, despite the society's drastic modernization process. Models show general trust does not perform differently in China than in Western countries, but remains positively associated with democracy. However, the impact of in-group particular trusts prove to be complex. Trust in colleagues and friends can facilitate democratic support, which can also encourage individual voting behaviors. The rest of the particular trust found in the discrete circles has nothing to do with democracy. In China, the previously identified "high-trust–low-democracy" puzzle can be largely explained by the failure to differentiate Chinese thick particular trust from general trust in standard measurement of trust in surveys.

The chapter proceeds as follows: I briefly review the literature on general trust, social trust, and democracy and those of social capital studies in China in the following section. Next, the theoretical arguments on the relations between trust and democracy under Confucian cultural tradition are presented. In the empirical test section, I first clarify the data sources, describe in detail the measurements of particular and general trust, democratic values, and other variables and justify the choices of statistical models, then I report and interpret the statistical models explaining the impact of trust on democratic values and voting in China. I conclude the chapter by discussing the implication of my findings and future trust research in China.

Literature Review: Social Capital and Democracy

Complaints on the vagueness of the concept of trust aside,[27] *social trust* is generally defined as the cultural perspective of social capital (Putnam 1995), "the expectation that arises within a community of regular, honest, and cooperative behavior, based on commonly shared norms, on the part of other members of that community" (Fukuyama 1995, 26). According to the wisdom inherited from the tradition of eighteenth-century Scottish moralists as well as modern democracy thinkers including John Locke, John Stuart Mill, and Alexis de Tocqueville, the establishment of new bonds of community and association based on the idea of trust is posited as one of the conditions of civilized democratic society. As the main component of social capital, social trust is a necessary condition for economic efficiencies and democratic consolidation. The "legitimation" of modern democratic society is founded on the "trust" in authority and in governments as the general trust in the primary, interpersonal level (Seligman 1997). Empirical examination

27 The critiques of the vagueness of the concept of trust are seen in many social capital literatures. For a review, see Kenneth Newton, "Trust, Social Capital, Civil Society, and Democracy," *International Political Science Review* 22 (2002): 201–21.

of social capital starts from the classic civic culture study by Almond and Verba (1963). Comparative data from five countries after World War II indicate that social trust has divergent impacts on political behaviors in those countries. Whereas social trust facilitates political trust and engagement in the United States and the United Kingdom, Almond and Verba observed no evidence of a positive influence of social trust on political attitudes and behaviors in Germany, Mexico, and Italy. However, not until Robert Putnam and Ronald Inglehart did the social capital theory start to occupy the center of civic culture studies. To explain the differing performance of governments in southern and northern Italy, Putnam and his coauthors (Putnam, Leonard, and Nanetti 1993) traced the civic roots of Italy and found social capital is associated with institutional success in northern Italy. They reached the famous conclusion that "Building social capital will not be easy, but it is the key to making democracy work" (Putnam et al. 1993, 185). Meanwhile, mostly based on his widely used databases of the World Values Survey (six waves so far), Inglehart has contributed to the literature of social capital by empirically demonstrating the positive association between interpersonal trust and level of democracy (Inglehart 1997; Inglehart and Welzel 2005). Both of the distinguished contributors to social capital theory have been criticized methodologically (e.g., Seligson 2002) and theoretically; however, this has not seemed to damage the comparatists' passion. Given that the third wave of democratization has reached almost every corner of the world, they are strongly motivated to extend the examination of theory to broader cultural background.

American political scientists originally studied the relationship between trust and democracy for the purpose of detecting the logic of American democracy. They read between the lines of de Tocqueville and discovered that he highly praised American democracy's characteristics of unique spirit of community and vigorous activities among civic associations, which directly connects with interpersonal trust. However, starting in the 1990s, American social scientists noticed a remarkable decline of US social capital (e.g., Putnam 1995; Skocpol and Fiorina 1999; Warren 1999). The decline of a "civic" generation since World War II was so obvious that it directly damaged Americans' political life and the United States as a democracy (Putnam 1995). Social capital studies in the United States quickly led to a series of comparative studies in other Western countries, including in-depth case studies in the Nordic region (e.g., Delhey and Newton 2005; Stolle 1998), the United Kingdom (Li, Pickles, and Savage 2005), Canada (Stolle, Soroka, and Johnston 2008), Japan (e.g., Freitag 2006), and regional and global large-N comparative studies (e.g., Delhey et al. 2011; Newton 2006; Zmerli and Newton 2008). Using various survey data, the line of literature mainly explores the relationships among trust, civic engagement, and political trust and examines what socioeconomic factors affect the building and consequences of social capital. The results are relatively stable in the Western setting; namely, social capital plays a crucial role in almost every dimension of democracy. In explaining the varying levels of social capital in diverse societies, factors such as ethnic homogeneity (or heterogeneity) and religions were found to be of significance (e.g., Delhey et al. 2011; Freitag 2006).

The basically positive association between trust and democracy in a Western setting ignites scholars' passion for applying the theory in emerging democracies and even in authoritarian regimes. Comparatists attempt to incorporate the concept of social capital into democratization theories, asking how trust can potentially affect the process of democratization. With the help of regional barometers, there have been cross-national trust studies conducted in central Eastern Europe (e.g., Letki and Evans 2005), Asia (e.g., Inoguchi 2004; Tan and Tambyah 2011) and in specific countries including Russia (e.g., Mishler and Rose 2005; Secor and O'Loughlin 2005), South Korea (e.g., Kawachi and Subramanian 2011; Kim 2005), and China (Chen and Lu 2007; Palmer, Perkins, and Xu 2011; Steinhardt 2012; Xu et al. 2010). Analyses show the complicated results when the trust theory travels. On the one hand, trust is shown to be generally relevant to democratic development (Inglehart 1997). However, unlike in advanced democracies, the impact of trust on democratic transition, consolidation, and the stability issue is empirically uncertain (e.g., Inglehart and Welzel 2005; Newton 2001; Roßteutscher 2010; Torcal and Montero 1999, 181). For example, the proposed positive relations among trust, political participation, and political trust fail to appear in democratizing Russia (Secor and O'Loughlin 2005) and South Korea (Kim 2005). On the other hand, these studies seek to explain trust as a dependent variable. For example, different from the Western bottom-up style of trust building, trust is shaped by state power at the top in post-communist countries (e.g., Freitag 2006; Letki and Evans 2005). The existing comparative studies in emerging democracies challenge the previous linear relation between trust and democracy, calling for a more careful examination of cultural elements in the process, including the Eastern Confucian societies.

Previous large-N studies on trust have somehow detected China as an outlying case in terms of the relationship between trust and democracy (e.g., Inglehart 1997; Seligson 2002, 278), a combination of a high level of trust and stalled democratic development. Logically, it could be due to theoretical and/or methodological reasons. Theoretically, the causal mechanism of trust on democracy could possibly be transformed due to unique Chinese factors. Methodologically, the trust questions in the existing surveys could have failed to accurately capture the level of Chinese trust. However, both of these possibilities are linked to the differentiation between particular trust and general trust (e.g., Gambetta 1988; Portes and Landolt 1996; Portes and Sensenbrenner 1993). The former is within family and based on face-to-face interaction among friends, whereas the latter happens by psychological connections without individuals personally knowing one another (Mishler and Rose 2005, 1053; Putnam 1995, 172). The differentiation of two types of trust are of great significance in the sense that what we call the "chicken soup" (Newton 2001; Putnam et al. 1993; Seligman 1997, 14; Uslaner 2002, 1) for democracy and better life basically refers to the general interpersonal trust, usually measured by a standard question in surveys: "Generally speaking, would you say that most people can be trusted or that you need to be very careful in dealing with people?" Noelle-Neumann first devised the question to measure an unfamiliar circle of others rather than a small circle of close and family others (Delhey et al. 2011, 788); therefore, this question does not reflect respondents' levels of particular trust or mistakenly mixes the two types of trust when gauging the level of interpersonal trust. Recently research by Delhey et al. (2011) addressed the problem by adding in a new dimension of trust, the radius of general trust specifically. Thanks to the sixth wave of the World Values Survey, which designed new batteries for trust measurement, Delhey et al. discovered the varying radius of general trust across the globe. However, the radius of trust problem remains unresolved (Delhey et al. 2014; van Hoorn 2014). Delhey and colleagues' research raises more questions than actually solving the problem. One is left wondering how the discovery of radius of trust fits the previous large body of trust literature. Now, we are even compelled to investigate particular trust, which has mostly been ignored in the literature (Newton and Zmerli 2011).

As a matter of fact, it is critically important to differentiate between particular trust and general trust and to look into the perspective of radius of trust in Confucian society. Confucianism sets up a stringent boundary between family members, friends, and outsiders that may directly affect the nature and structure of interpersonal trust. In this perspective, current Chinese scholars mostly focus on the question of what factors can be associated with the pattern of Chinese trust (e.g., Bo 2003; Li and Liang 2002; Ma 2007; Tong and Qu 2010; Wang and Liu 2002; Yan 2006; Yang and Peng 1999; Zhai 2009). Few scholars have empirically investigated the relationship between trust and political attitudes and behaviors in China (e.g., Feng 2007; Long 2012), which is what this chapter aims to do. By including the well-known concept of *Cha Xu Ge Ju* (differential mode of social networks) by Fei Xiaotong [28] into the analysis, I will first demonstrate the differential pattern of trust in China and then calculate the impact of trusts on Chinese democratic values and political participation.

Theories: General Trust, Particular Trust, and Democracy

Trust and Democracy

Why is trust the chicken soup for modern democracy? What are the causal mechanisms of trust on the functioning of democracy? Theorists have basically generalized three linkages between trust and democracy.

28 See the recently translated version of Fei Xiaotong, *From the Soil: The Foundations of Chinese Society*. Beijing: Foreign Language Teaching and Research Press, 2012.

First, elections and other institutions in a representative democracy rely on trust from loyal oppositions who equally accept the game rules of democracy. Modern representative democracies are based on free and fair elections. With elections, there are winners and losers; that is, power alternation among political parties that represent diverse social groups is one of the key features of modern representative democracies (Cheibub 2007, 26; Dahl 1971, 1). "The loyal opposition[s]" (Inglehart 1997, 54) is indispensable for democracy to work. A well-functioning democracy requires loyal opposition(s) to trust their opponents when being defeated in democratic competitions. Trust is the conviction that the opponent shares the same set of beliefs that everyone has another chance to access power on the basis of democratic principles. This is a belief that the oppositions will not be repressed in the next round of competition, a belief that the incumbent will step down when losing the election, and a belief that the oppositions do not need to become violent to get rid of the government if it violates democratic rules. Therefore, given this trust, opponents are inclined to cooperate within the boundary of the democratic rule of competition. Essentially, trust helps to connect people who are different from one another and ultimately generates compromise within society (Uslaner 2002, 190), a core value for democratic operation (Dahl 1971).

Second, social capital theorists argue that by improving voluntary association, social trust facilitates an active and cooperative civil society, which is an indispensable condition for a consolidated democratic society (e.g., Kim et al. 2012; Kwak et al.

2004; Mishler and Rose 2005; Putnam 1993, 1995, 2000; Uslaner 2002). The sense of a common set of beliefs within the community usually goes hand in hand with citizens' engagement in voluntary association. A trusting civil society is a cooperative society in which all people share a set of ideas, which helps to resolve the problem of collective activity. When people trust others, they are more willing to participate in charities and volunteer their time and resources. This civic engagement in turn reinforces interpersonal trust by increasing the costs to a defector, fostering robust norms of reciprocity, and improving the flow of information (Putnam 1995, 173–174). A trusting citizen is more likely to discuss politics and be vigorously involved in political activities. Behind civic engagements based on general interpersonal trust are horizontal interactions and equivalent status among people. More important, general trust is perhaps a weaker tie compared with dense kinship or patron-client bonds, but this relatively weak tie has its strength (Granovetter 1973) in that it can spread to a much broader social sphere and promise social exchange networks among the entire community, which should foster institutional success and good governance at the community level.

Third, interpersonal trust is also argued to have a "spill over" effect, indirectly enhancing citizens' trust in political institutions (Mishler and Rose 2005); explicitly, face-to-face interpersonal trust can spill over to cooperation at the community level as well as "spill up," contributing to trust in the representatives of institutions (Mishler and Rose 2005; Putnam 1993). In a representative democracy, voters cast their trust in the chosen representatives through elections. They trust the selected agents who will fight for their interests. Even in the case of choosing irresponsible ones, the voters remain confident that the democratic rules will deliver the possibility to get rid of them fairly. Ultimately, trust in political institutions contributes to the citizens' commitment to democracy and promotes democratic stability. In short, in established democracies, one should observe a natural mixture of interpersonal and political trusts.

Particular Trust in Confucian Tradition: The Ripplelike Pattern

However, the aforementioned three mechanisms are essentially based on general trust, the belief that most people can be trusted even if one does not know them personally and even if they have social differences (Newton and Zmerli 2011, 171). In contrast, particular trust, no matter whether it is defined in "knowledge-based" or "own-kind" styles, is largely associated with specific, known people or in-group others (Hardin 2001, 34). It is characteristically a basis of strong and high-density ties in a relatively narrow-scale fashion. In fact, the sharp contrast between in-groups and out-groups defines one of the most salient features of Confucianism. Thus, to study trust in China, one has to consider the consequences of cultural tradition.

The most salient influence of Confucianism on trust perhaps derives from familism, the central feature in the moral life for everyone in Confucian society (Ebrey 2014). The core of what Tu Weiming (1998) calls "Confucian personal ethic" is the concept of family (*jia* in Chinese), which carries almost full ethnic meanings in Confucian societies. Of the five cardinal relationships,[29] the father-son relationship is key, for it establishes the moral obligation of *Xiao*, or filial piety, which is Confucianism's central moral imperative (Fukuyama 1995; Yao 2000; Tu 1998). Sons have obligations to defer to their parents' authority. Children show their respect and *Xiao* to parents by complying with their wishes and following their teachings, whether in terms of everyday life or crucial life decisions. In traditional Chinese society, rebellions against parents are unthinkable. Challenging parents' authority is treated as a lack of filial piety. When parents get old, sons have the unconditional duty to provide economic support. The other side of solid family bonds is the parents' dedication and sacrifices for their children. In Confucian scholars' eyes, parents also have the obligation to do everything they can to economically support children for their education, marriage, and even helping them raise the grandchildren. It is often noted that the parents in Confucian society are anxious to see their children married and accumulate property. Parents work hard and live thriftily so they can save capital for future generations (Ebrey 2014).

29 Confucianism emphasizes five cardinal hierarchical affiliations (*Wulun*) between the monarch and his subjects, father and son, husband and wife, elder brother and younger brother, and between friends,

Implied in this solid parent-child bond are the characteristic ideas and practice of the family system. This, on the one hand, suggests there is no such thing as individualism in the Confucian ethnic; that is, individuals' behaviors are legitimate only if they are made in the name of family, for the honor, the prosperity, the reputation, and everything of the family. On the other land, familism suggests that Confucian morality, including piety, obligation, and loyalties, is developed within the boundary of family.

When emphasizing filial piety and obligations to the family, the obligations and duties to anyone outside the family[30] are noticeably weak (Fukuyama 1995). A clear line between the family and outsiders comes into being. Family members are family members. Strangers are strangers.[31] Even though modern Confucian societies have distinguished themselves from conventional ones by loosening the family line, the emphasis on interpersonal familiarity based on the face-to-face interaction remains. In other words, when the concept of in-groups is extended to friends and other groups people are familiar with and not restricted to family members, the differentiation between in-groups and out-groups is still of great importance. Unlike Westerners, Easterners feel embedded in the in-groups and distant from the out-groups (Nisbett 2003). Keeping

---

30 Family in Confucian society is visibly different from the Western family, a much broader concept exceeding the scope of the nuclear family.

31 This line could be very easily noticed in daily life in East Asian society. For example, it is utterly strange and silly to say hello to or smile at strangers when walking down Chinese streets. One is only supposed to do this with those who are familiar.

in mind the clear line between insiders and outsiders, people seek social exchanges and build reciprocity among family members and friends. Dense social networks are developed mostly among in-groups. If interpersonal interactions generate information about the trustworthiness of other actors (Putnam 1995, 172), interactions happening within in-groups generate trust therein. By the same token, a lack of communication and interaction with outsiders produces a weak trust in them. As famously argued by Fei Xiaotong, "Social relationships in China possess a self-centered quality. Like the ripples formed from a stone thrown into a lake, each circle spreading out from the center becomes more distant and at the same time more insignificant" (Fei 2012, 46). Thus, what the Confucian school has called *Renlun* (human relationships) is a term to describe Chinese social relationships, signifying "the ripplelike effect created from circles of relationships that spread out from the self, an effect that produces a pattern of discrete circles." Thus, we cannot assume that traditional Confucian trust based on face-to-face interaction can directly "spill over" (Mishler and Rose 2005) to others in general. It is more reasonable to hypothesize a ripplelike pattern of trust in China.

Particular Trust and Democracy

Now reconsider the causal mechanisms of trust on democracy from the perspective of particular trust. First, does *Cha Xu Ge Ju* in the Confucian tradition facilitate loyal oppositions? Democratic competitions at the country level are largely beyond the in-group boundary. When people with Confucian values tend to form social networks, pursue interests, and seek social exchanges among in-groups, it is a challenge indeed for them to trust an opponent who is normally an outsider. I am not arguing that it is impossible to have loyal oppositions in Confucian society—obviously, the democratic case of Taiwan does—but it is not unreasonable to assume that people embracing more particular trust, in order to establish psychological connections with political opponents, require more efforts to overcome the barrier inherited in their tradition. Second, particular trust is associated more with vertical networks and hierarchical relationships among people within in-groups. In this matter, interpersonal exchanges and reciprocal obligations are lopsided and asymmetric on the one hand and limited and unevenly spread among community on the other. The emphasis on hierarchical order in Confucian values implies the solid family bond is developed more on interpersonal dependence than mutuality because the resources and power are unevenly distributed and controlled. From this perspective, particular trust is substantially different from general trust in that it derives more from obedience to authority as well as the filial piety and obligations in hierarchical interpersonal relationships. To be fair, this kinship to some extent does resolve some problems of collective activity (as noticed in Asian family-based business)—namely, the trust based on vertical networks can generate collaboration—but this collaboration does not overcome the gap between in-groups and out-groups. The cooperation still dwells within the boundary of in-groups, which does not generate cooperative and independent civil associations at the community level but only collaboration limitedly based on the bonds of blood. Third, as I argued in a previous section, we cannot assume that dense particular trust can easily spill over to strangers, much less "spill up" to political institutions. By the same token, it is doubtful that without enough democratic learning experiences, people with particular trust feel psychologically connected with representatives who are mostly outsiders. They may trust the political leaders due to the elitist orientations in the Confucian tradition (Shin and Wells 2005; Pye 1992; Pye and Pye 1985; Yao 2000), but this could further damage the "spill up" effect to political institutions.

In short, it is imperative to differentiate between particular trust and general trust in Confucian societies. Whereas general trust theoretically has positive impacts on democracy, particular trust may fail to encourage democratic values in countries with a Confucian tradition. China with *Cha Xu Ge Ju*, a differential mode of interpersonal relations and social network, is hypothesized to show a differential model of trust as well as differential impacts on democracy. Now I depend on the raw data collected in China to empirically examine the hypotheses. More important, I am especially interested in the boundary of in-groups and out-groups in current China.

Research Design: Data, Measurement, and Statistical Models

China held the latest local People's Congress elections in early 2012. Taking advantage of the once-in-five-years opportunity, we conducted a survey right after the election in the city of Nanjing, a metropolis located in southeast China with a population of more than six million people. The choice of Nanjing had both practical and theoretical reasons. In practice, Nanjing is one of only two cities in China (the other is Shanghai) that for the first time employed an electronic registration system in the election. This system has full information for about 5.6 million voters, which provided us the unprecedented chance to conduct random sampling. Also, as the location of my university, Nanjing was more convenient for our hired interviewers, mostly students from Nanjing University, to conduct the survey. Theoretically, megacities in China such as Nanjing are more likely modernized, in which case, if we still can detect the differential mode of trust implied in the Confucian tradition, we would be even more confident about applying the finding to less modernized rural areas. We sampled 2,399 cases and successfully conducted 1,199 interviews with the efforts of our team.[32]

32 Thanks to my colleagues Dr. Xiaobo Lu and Dr. Jingping Lai from the School of Government at Nanjing University, who are the other two chief coordinators of the survey project.

Cha Xu Ge Ju: Describing the Ripplelike Mode of Trust in Urban China

The measurement of trusts in our survey depends on this question: "*On a 1 (*low*) to 10 (*high*) scale, how much trust do you have in each of the following types of people? Family members, relatives and friends, schoolmates, those who are introduced by relatives and friends, colleagues, others (strangers)?*" Table 1, Table 2, and Figure 1 show a solid differential pattern of interpersonal trust in Nanjing. Here, the citizens' average trust level in family members reaches 9.58 points (10 possible); 78% of all respondents trust their family 100%; adding the 12.45% who scored 9 points, we find that 90% of all people unconditionally trust their family. However, the level of trust decreases and the variations of trust levels increase with the extension of concentric circles of social networks. The average level of trust in relatives and friends declines to 8.7 points; schoolmates, 7.7; acquaintances, 6.9; colleagues, 6.8; and strangers, only 4.2. Regarding Nanjingers' trust in strangers, 67.27% scored fewer than 5 points and 17.48%, only 1 point. Table 2 reports the comparative scores of trust in families versus strangers on the 1 to 10 scale, which reveals a sharp contrast between families and outsiders. Furthermore, the *Cha Xu Ge Ju* of trust is not only reflected in the average trust in different groups of people but also the increasing variations (see Column 4, Table 1). Specifically, if Chinese largely show consensus on family trust, the personal differences in trust levels increase and widen as others are more and more distant in the discrete circles. Then, what is the structure of each individual's trust? What portion of total trust is assigned to general trust in strangers?

Table 1. **The Differential Modes of Trust in Urban China**

Trust	N	Average	Standard Deviation	Minimum	Maximum
Family Members	1,141	9.58	1.03	1	10
Relatives & Friends	1,127	8.70	1.38	1	10
Schoolmates	1,036	7.76	1.57	1	10
Acquaintances	1,080	6.92	1.76	1	10
Colleagues	1,052	6.80	1.89	1	10
Others (Strangers)	1,087	4.28	2.22	1	10

Figure 1. The Discrete Circles of Trust in China

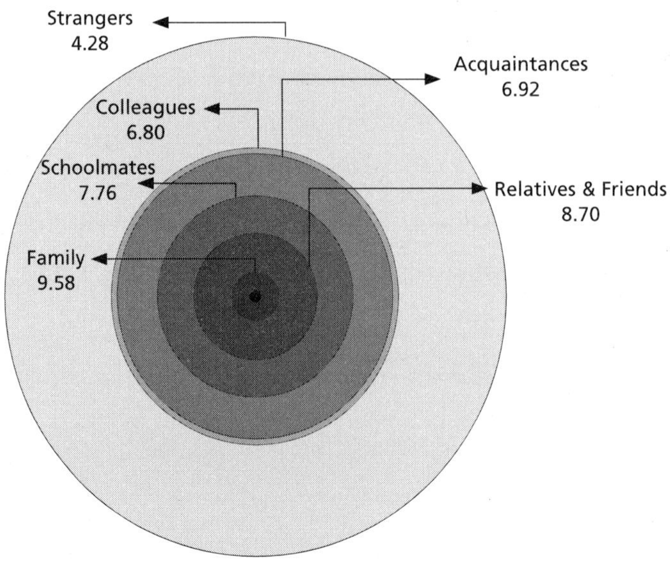

Table 2. **Frequencies of Trust in Family and Trust in Strangers**

Score	Trust in Family		Trust in Strangers	
	Frequency	Percentage	Frequency	Percentage
1	3	0.26%	190	17.48%
2	1	0.09	92	8.46
3	1	0.09	120	11.04
4	3	0.26	106	9.75
5	11	0.96	245	22.54
6	8	0.70	166	15.27
7	15	1.31	93	8.56
8	67	5.87	53	4.88
9	142	12.45	12	1.10
10	890	78	10	0.92
Total	1141	100	1087	100

Pearson $\chi^2(81) = 90.59$, p-value = 0.2

Table 3. **The Differential Modes of Trust for Individuals (N = 970)**

Trust	Average Percentage	Standard Deviation	Minimum	Maximum
Family	0.220	0.036	0.05	0.52
Relatives & Friends	0.198	0.028	0.02	0.38
Schoolmates	0.176	0.026	0.03	0.64
Acquaintances	0.156	0.031	0.03	0.30
Colleagues	0.151	0.031	0.19	0.29
Strangers	0.097	0.044	0.19	0.45

Figure 2: The Differential Modes of Trust for Individuals (N = 970)

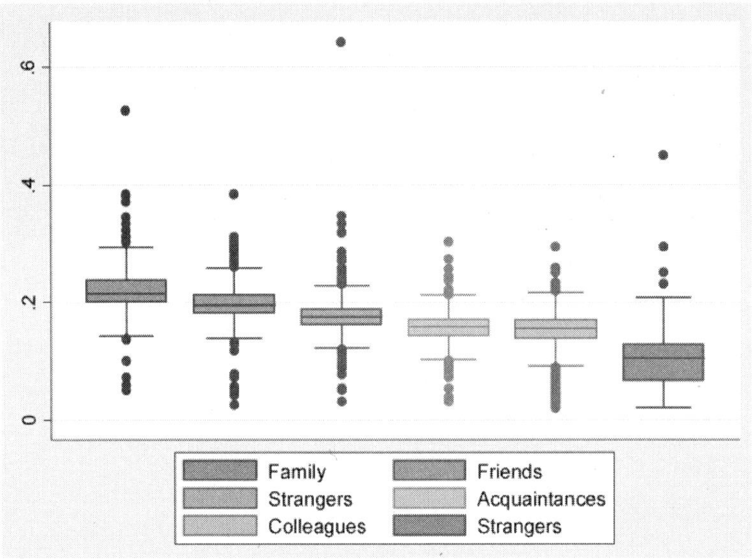

As reported in Table 3 and Figure 2, the portion of trust assigned to different groups also decreases progressively from families to strangers. On average, Nanjingers' trust in strangers is only 9%; that is, if someone scores a total of 10 points of trust in others, only 1 point is assigned to trust in strangers. See Table 2 for detailed data of proportions for each group, which echoes the pattern shown in Tables 1 and 2: Both at the aggregate level and the individual level, differential trust circles are identified for Chinese patterns of trust. This finding speaks to Delhey and colleagues' calculation where China is a typical case of a small radius of general trust combined with a high level of total trust (Delhey et al. 2011, 793-794). On the basis of our data, this high level of Chinese interpersonal trust can be largely explained from the prevailing and persistent particular trust that is entrenched in Confucian tradition. We find it is interesting that the drastic pace of modernization in urban areas of today's China, in such megacities as Nanjing, seems to fail to fundamentally transform and erode the tradition. The traditional discrete circles of social networks prove resilient, which leaves us a distinct Chinese pattern of trust.

One more detail from the data is worthy of discussion. In China, the interpersonal trust among schoolmates is fairly high, right next to relatives. In contrast, for Chinese, the colleagues with whom they spend most of their time seem not quite as trustworthy, better than only strangers. Intense interactions do not seem to necessarily lead Chinese to trust others. This is possibly because people tend to be more cautious when personal interests are deeply involved in the workplace, whereas school friendships are largely independent of such interests.

General Trust, Particular Trust, and Democracy in China

How are the differential circles of trust associated with Chinese democratic values? I depend on multivariate regression models to calculate the relations. By referring to the mainstream measurement on democracy in established literatures, databases, and surveys (e.g., Munck and Verkulien 2002; also see World Values Surveys and regional barometers), we designed three questions: *"Do you strongly agree (*1 point*), somewhat agree, somewhat disagree, or strongly disagree (*4 points*): a) democracy is always preferable to any other kind of government; b) Democracy is capable of solving the problems of our society; c) democracy is more important than economic development."* I added the points given for each of the three questions and recalculated them on a 1 to 100 scale. Higher scores imply higher levels of democratic support. Literatures show that democratic support also depends on other control variables, including 1) the behavioral dimension of social capital, civic engagement, measured by a dichotomous variable from a question of *"Are you a member of any organization or formal group (such as trade association, labor union, or sports or leisure club, etc.)*?" (1 = yes, 0 = no). 2) Evaluation of government performances is regarded as an important source of democratic support (e.g., Anderson and Guillory 1997; Evans and Whitefield 1995; Mishler and Rose 2005; Norris 1999). The respondent's answer to the question of "*On the whole, are you satisfied (*1*) or dissatisfied (*0*) with the way democracy works in our country?*" is used as the measurement for this variable. 3) Confidence in political institutions. Theoretically, those who are confident about democratic institutions are more likely to be supportive of democracy as a regime, whereas confidence in authoritarian institutions may have a negative effect on democratic support. This variable depends on the question *"To what extent are you confident about political institutions (such as municipal* *government, official organizations in the communities, etc.)?* 4) Political experiences prove to be an important source of preference for democracy (e.g., Mattes and Bratton 2007). We asked in the questionnaire, *"In the past several years, have you been involved in the following activities: contact the directors in your workplace to solve your problems; contact government officials; contact Chinese Communist Party organizations; petition; discuss politics online; contact media; contact nongovernment organizations for help; protest the officials; sue the officials; and demonstration."* For each item, yes scores 1, no scores 0, and the total score reflects the points for the variable of participation. 5) On the basis of the Asian Value debates, Confucianism could be negatively (or positively) associated with democratic values (e.g., Bell 2005; Shin 2012; Zakaria 1994). I measure Confucianism according to the following dimensions: collectivism (*"Do you agree that we should sacrifice our individual interest for the sake of the collective interest?"*; authority (*"Even if parents' demands are unreasonable, children still should do what they ask."*); familism (*"For the sake of the family, the individual should put his personal interests second"*); individualism (*"Individuals should not exhibit themselves even if they are capable and knowledgeable."*); hierarchicalism (*"When conflicts occur in the family, the older people needs to be invited to mediate."*). 6) Given China's characteristic political regimes, I add two more variables, CCP membership and national pride. For the former, I further argue that it has an interactive effect with regime evaluation on the democratic support; that is, as the hard core of the Chinese communist system, CCP members' positive evaluation of the regime may lead to the rejection of alternative regimes. National pride, measured by the question *"Are you proud of being Chinese?"* could potentially improve their recognition of the current regime and cast doubt on the suitability of alternatives. 7) Last is a group of demographic variables, including gender (man = 1), age, education, and income. See the appendix for the descriptive data for all variables. On the basis of the data, I adopted a regression with robust standard error to explain democratic support. Considering the possible influences of outlying cases, I tested all models with robust regression for the model robustness. See Table 4 for the reported results.

Table 4. **Regression with Robust Standard Error Explaining Democratic Support**

	Model 1	Model 2	Model 3	Model 4	Model 5	Model 6
Trust Family	0.13(0.44)					
Trust Friends		0.70(0.42)*				
Trust Schoolmates			−0.04(0.39)			
Trust Acquaintances				0.45(0.32)		
Trust Colleagues					0.67(0.38)*	
Trust Strangers					.	0.45(0.26)*
Civic Engagement	−2.29(1.76)	−2.42 (1.75)	−2.10(1.83)	−1.80 (1.85)	−1.58 (1.78)	−2.32(1.86)
Regime Satisfaction	0.03(0.44)	0.001 (0.44)	0.28 (0.46)	−0.02 (0.45)	0.16 (0.45)	−0.03(0.45)
Chinese Communist Party (CCP)	7.64(4.08)*	7.63 (4.08)*	8.38 (4.15)*	7.52 (4.10)*	8.55 (4.07)*	6.94(4.14)*
Regime Sat *CCP	−0.76(0.63)***	−1.75 (0.63)**	−1.88 (0.65)**	−1.77 (0.63)**	−1.86 (0.63)**	−1.62(0.65)**
Political Trust	−0.06(0.12)	−0.09(0.12)	−.10(0.12)	−.06(0.12)	−0.18(0.12)	−.10(0.12)
Political Participation	0.39(0.37)	0.47(0.36)	.37(0.40)	0.46(0.36)	0.45(0.37)	0.38(0.37)
National Pride	−1.85(0.93)*	−1.75(0.92)*	−2.22(0.97)*	−1.91(0.94)*	−1.88(0.94)*	−1.92(0.93)*
Confucianism	1.17(0.26)***	1.12(0.27)***	1.15(0.28)***	1.04(0.27)***	1.08(0.27)***	1.05(0.27)***
Age	0.12(0.03)***	0.12(0.03)***	.11(0.03)**	0.11(0.03)***	0.11(0.03)**	0.13(0.03)***
Gender	1.19(0.97)	1.13(0.96)	1.48(1.00)	1.32(.98)	1.32(0.98)	1.25(0.98)
Education	−1.38(0.64)*	−1.41(0.65)*	−1.38(0.72)*	−1.30(.67)*	−1.29(0.66)*	−1.5(0.65)*
Income	0.61(0.57)	0.66(0.57)	0.82(0.57)	0.67(.57)	0.59(0.56)	0.58(0.57)
Constant	40.45(6.99)	36.66(6.65)	42.51(6.46)	40.57(6.32)	39.35(6.20)	43.08(6.17)
N	809	806	751	779	764	785
R-Square	0.1335	0.1341	0.1239	0.1206	0.1253	0.1308

Note: Entries are unstandardized ordinary least squares regression coefficients with standard errors in parentheses.
*p<0.1, **p<0.05, ***p<0.01.

Results in Table 4 largely confirm the revealed differential mode of trust discussed herein, but more important, it shows the interesting effects of Chinese trust. With a series of control variables, trust in strangers (Model 6, Table 4), the very outer circle of trust, proves to have a statistically positive effect on democratic values, which echoes the findings from the existing literature; namely, general trust is positively associated with democracy. However, more than that, in China, the trust in colleagues and coworkers (Model 5), like that in strange others, also shows a similar effect on democratic support. Thus, in terms of the relationship between trust and democracy, the radius of general trust in China can be extended to the trust in colleagues. The psychological connections built in the working environment in China share similar mechanisms with trust toward strangers. Different from the patterns of particular trust, including that in family, schoolmates, and acquaintances, colleagues are utterly regarded as outsiders by Chinese. The particular trusts (Models 1, 3, and 4; Table 4) fail to gain statistical significance in predicting democratic support, which also confirms the hypotheses on the trust-democracy relationship in the Confucian tradition. However, there is a surprise in Table 4: the effect of the trust in friends and relatives. The variable of this typical in-group trust in the differential circles is unexpectedly associated with democratic support, which may imply more complexity in the influence of particular trust in this society, as reported in recent research (e.g., Cao et al. 2015). In terms of the trust-democracy relationship, the findings about China shown in Table 4 are both a confirmation and a challenge for the general social capital theory. It is a confirmation because general trust remains significant for democracy and particular trust largely remains disconnected from democracy in China. It is a challenge because the radius of Chinese general trust can somehow spread to in-groups, such as colleagues and coworkers. In addition, the unpredicted effect of trust on friends calls for more examination of the structure of particular trust.

Table 4 also reports interesting results regarding control variables. The coefficient of the interactive item of CCP membership and satisfaction with regime is statistically significant. Take Model 1 as an example: The coefficient of regime satisfaction is 0.29, CCP membership 8.31, and the interactive item is −1.80. I recalculate the coefficients to interpret the effects of these two variables. Specifically, if an individual is not a CCP member (CCP = 0), regime satisfaction is positively related to democratic support but gains no significance statistically. If a person is a member (CCP = 1), then the coefficient of regime satisfaction becomes −1.51. So, the more satisfied a CCP member is with the current Chinese regime, the less he or she is prone to be democratic, which illustrates that Chinese with vested interests are more likely to reject alternative regimes. The significance of this effect is rather stable, as reported across all six models in Table 4. The models also show that citizens' civic engagement and political participative activities can both lead to a higher level of democratic support, although the effect of the latter is not that stable. National pride has a negative impact on Chinese democratic values. The more proud one is of being Chinese, the less he or she is fond of democracy. It is interesting that our data show that Confucian culture facilitates democratic support, whereas education hinders democratic values, findings that are in conflict with the existing literatures. One possible explanation is that Chinese may have a different interpretation of the concept of democracy. As with trust, we also need to reexamine the connotation of democracy under different cultural circumstances.

I previously analyzed how trust is associated with democratic values. To reveal the mechanisms, I further examine how trust influences individuals' political activities by using multivariate regressions to explain their voting behaviors. The dependent variable is dichotomous, as measured by whether individuals cast votes in the local People's Congress elections (voted = 1; did not vote = 0). Because the dependent variable here is dichotomous, I chose to use a logistic model with robust standard error and included the related control variables (see the appendix for descriptive data).

Table 5. **Logistic Regression Explaining Voting in Local People's Congress Election**

	Model 1	Model 2	Model 3	Model 4	Model 5	Model 6
Trust Family	0.01(0.06)					
Trust Friends		0.09(0.05)*				
Trust Schoolmates			0.04(0.04)			
Trust Acquaintances				0.03(0.04)		
Trust Colleagues					0.001(0.04)	
Trust Strangers						0.08(0.03)**
Civic Engagement	0.80(0.16)**	0.86(.27)**	0.73(.27)**	0.73(.27)**	0.74(.27)**	0.73(.28)**
Regime Satisfaction	0.01(00)*	0.01(00)	0.01(00)*	0.01(00)*	0.01(00)*	0.01(00)*
Corruption	−0.09(0.04)*	−0.08(0.04)*	−0.08(0.04)*	−0.08(0.04)*	−0.08(0.04)	−0.07(0.04)*
Chinese Communist Party (CCP)	0.50(0.18)**	0.52(0.18)**	0.59(0.20)**	0.53(0.19)**	0.53(0.19)**	0.50(0.19)**
Political Knowledge	0.04(0.05)	0.03(0.05)	0.04(0.05)	0.04(0.05)	0.04(0.05)	0.03(0.05)
Political Discussion	0.26(0.09)**	0.25(0.09)**	0.30(0.10)**	0.26(0.09)**	0.25(0.09)**	0.26(0.09)**
Political Efficacy	−0.01(00)*	0.12(0.09)	0.14(0.09)	0.11(0.09)	0.16(0.09)	0.18(0.09)*
Participation Experiences	0.05(0.04)	0.06(0.04)	0.04(0.04)	0.06(0.04)	0.06(0.04)	0.05(0.04)
Age	−0.01(00)	−0.01(00)*	−0.01(00)*	−0.01(00)*	−0.01(.00)**	−0.01(00)*
Gender	−0.21(0.14)	−0.21(0.14)	−0.25(0.15)*	−0.17(0.15)	−0.20(0.15)	−0.22(0.15)
Education	0.14(0.09)*	0.14(0.09)	0.13(0.10)	0.18(0.09)*	0.15(0.09)*	0.13(0.09)
Income	−0.38(0.08)***	−0.38(0.08)***	−0.39(0.09)***	−0.40(0.09)***	−0.37(0.09)***	−0.38(0.08)***
Constant	−1.00(0.97)	−1.67(0.85)	−1.29(0.83)	−1.33(0.78)	−1.12(0.80)	−1.44(0.78)
N	908	899	830	863	842	867
Pseudo R-Square	0.0832	0.0863	0.0925	0.0882	0.0911	0.09336

Note: Entries are unstandardized ordinary least squares regression coefficients with standard errors in parentheses.
$*p<0.1$, $**p<0.05$, $***p<0.01$.

Results reported in Table 5 again confirmed the different impacts of Chinese general trust and particular in-group trusts on their political participation in general. Nanjingers with a higher level of general trust were more likely to vote for local representatives, whereas those who trust their family, schoolmates, acquaintances, and colleagues more were not more motivated to cast votes. Different from the effect on democratic support reported in Table 4, trust in colleagues loses the statistical significance on voting behaviors. The radius of general trust in Table 5 fails to extend toward any in-groups. So, if trust in colleagues can facilitate Chinese having positive attitudes toward democracy as an ideal regime, it does not necessarily encourage them to be more actively involved in political activities such as voting. Given that voting in present-day China carries little substantial meaning as a democratic practice, it is another interesting question whether the radius of trust can reach this circle of trust in other democratic activities. However, here, the variable of trust in relatives and friends again is statistically significant. Tables 4 and 5 both show that trust in friends in China is positively associated with both democratic values and voting activities. The unusual performance of this variable remains in Table 5 calls to further investigate the possible connection between particular trust and democracy in Confucian society.

Conclusion

For comparativists, the resilience of authoritarianism in China is an unresolved puzzle. This chapter explores one of the predictors of democracy, interpersonal trust, in China, and also aims to explain the identified Chinese high-trust–low-democracy dilemma. From the perspective of Confucian cultural tradition, ripplelike discrete circles of trust were discovered on the basis of our recent survey data. Current Chinese, even in highly modernized areas, remain heavily influenced by the traditional differential mode of social exchange networks. They show unconditional trust primarily in family members, and this trust becomes more and more distant and less and less significant as it spreads from the center to strangers. Models show that the variable of general trust does not perform unusually in China, which can both generate positive attitudes toward democracy and facilitate voting behaviors of Chinese in local elections. However, the complexion of the impacts of particular trust was also revealed. Trust in family members, schoolmates, and acquaintances has no positive influence on democracy. Trust in colleagues helps with affection for democracy but does not encourage voting. Most salient is the variable of trust in friends, a typical in-group trust, which is positively associated with both democratic values and activities.

The analyses herein suggest possible explanations for the high-trust–low-democracy puzzle. The high level of Chinese trust can be mainly attributed to the dense particular trust in Chinese trust circles, which was not identified by previous standard trust questions. Our data echoes the Delhey et al. (2011) finding of China as a case of a short radius of general trust combined with a high level of total trust. Although general trust remains the chicken soup for democracy in China, it has such a short radius that it can hardly challenge the differential mode of trust in this Confucian society. Ultimately, the good news is that Chinese tradition does not alter the functioning of general trust on democracy; the bad news is we only noticed a small portion of general trust among the discrete circles of trust in this Confucian society. In order to make trust good for democracy, Chinese have to overcome the cultural barriers entrenched in their tradition, which is not impossible but never seems easy.

References

References in English

Almond, Gabriel, and Sidney Verba.1963. *The Civil Culture: Political Attitudes and Democracy in Five Countries*. Princeton, NJ: Princeton University.

Anderson, Christopher, and Christian Guillory. 1997. "Political Institutions and Satisfaction with Democracy: A Cross-national Analysis of Consensus and Majoritarian Systems." *American Political Science Review* 91 (1): 66–81.

Bell, Daniel A. 2005. *Beyond Liberal Democracy*. Princeton, NJ: Princeton University Press.

Cao, Liqun, Jihong Zhao, and Ling Ren. 2015. "Do In-Group and Out-Group Forms of Trust Matter in Predicting Confidence in the Order Institutions? A Study of Three Culturally Distinct Countries." *International Sociology* 30 (6): 674-693.

Cheibub, Jose Antonio. 2007. *Presidentialism, Parliamentarism, and Democracy*. New York: Cambridge University Press.

Chen, Jie, and Chunlong Lu. 2007. "Social Capital in Urban China: Attitudinal and Behavioral Effects on Grassroots Self-Government." *Social Science Quarterly* 88 (2): 422-442.

Cook, Karen S. 2001. *Trust in Society*. New York: Russell Sage Foundation.

Dahl, Robert A. 1971. *Polyarchy: Participation and Opposition*. New Haven, CT: Yale University Press.

Delhey, Jan, and Kenneth Newton. 2005. "Predicting Cross-levels of Social Trust: Global Pattern or Nordic Exceptionalism."

European Sociological Review 21 (4): 311-327.

Delhey, Jan, Kenneth Newton, and Christian Welzel. 2011. "How General Is Trust in 'Most People'? Solving the Radius of Trust Problem." *American Sociological Review* 76 (5): 786-807.

Delhey, Jan, Kenneth Newton, and Christian Welzel. 2014. "The Radius of Trust Problem Remains Resolved." *American Sociological Review* 79 (6): 1260-1265.

Ebrey, Patricia Buckley. 2014. Confucianism and Family Rituals in Imperial China. Princeton, NJ: Princeton University Press.

Evans, Geoffrey, and Stephen Whitefield. 1995. "The Politics and Economics of Democratic Commitment: Support for Democracy in Transition Societies." *British Journal of Political Science* 25 (4): 485-514.

Fei, Xiaotong. 2012. *From the Soil: The Foundations of Chinese Society*. Beijing: Foreign Language Teaching and Research Press.

Freitag, Markus. 2006. "Bowling the State Back in: Political Institutions and the Creation of Social Capital." *European Journal of Political Research* 45 (1): 123-152.

Fukuyama, Francis. 1995. "Confucianism and Democracy." *Journal of Democracy* 6 (2): 20-33.

Gambetta, Diego. 1988. "Mafia: The Piece of Distrust." in *Trust: Making and Breaking Cooperative Relations*, edited by D. Gambetta, 158-175. Oxford, UK: Blackwell.

Glanville, Jennifer L., and Pamela Paxton. 2007. "How Do We Learn to Trust? A Confirmatory Tetrad Analysis of the Sources of Generalized Trust." *Social Psychology Quarterly* 70 (3): 230-242.

Granovetter, Mark S. 1973. "The Strength of Weak Ties." *The American Journal of Sociology* 78 (6): 1360-1380.

Hardin, Russell. 2001. "Conception and Explanations of Trust." In *Trust in Society*, edited by Karen S. Cook, 3-39. New York: Russell Sage Foundation.

Inglehart, Ronald. 1997. *Modernization and Post-modernization: Culture, Economic and Political Change in 43 Societies*. Princeton, NJ: Princeton University Press.

Inglehart, Ronald, and Christian Welzel. 2005. *Modernization, Culture Change and Democracy: The Human Development Sequence*. New York: Cambridge University Press.

Inoguchi, Takashi. 2004. "Social Capital in Ten Asian Societies." *Japanese Journal of Political Science* 5 (1): 197-211.

Jamal, Amaney, and Irfan Nooruddin. 2010. "The Democratic Utility of Trust: A Cross-national Analysis." *The Journal of Politics* 72 (1): 45-59.

Kim, Ji-Young, 2005. "'Bowling Together' Isn't a Cure-All: The Relationship between Social Capital and Political Trust in South Korea." *International Political Science Review* 26 (2): 193-213.

Kim, Seung-Sup, Yeonseung Chung, Melissa J. Perry, Ichiro Kawachi, and S.V. Subramanian. 2012. "Association Between Interpersonal Trust, Reciprocity, and Depression in South Korea: A Prospective Analysis." *PLoS ONE* 7 (1): 1-8.

Kwak, Nojin, Dhavan V. Shah, and R. Lance Holbert. 2004. "Connecting, Trusting, and Participating: The Direct and Interactive Effects of Social Associations." *Political Research Quarterly* 57 (4): 643-652.

Letki, Natalia, and Geoffrey Evans. 2005. "Endogenizing Social Trust:

Democratization in East-Central Europe." *British Journal Political Science* 35 (3): 515-529.

Li, Yaojun, Andrew Pickles, and Mike Savage. 2005. "Social Capital and Social Trust in Britain." *European Sociological Review* 21 (2): 109-123.

Maloy, J. S. 2009. "Two Concepts of Trust." *The Journal of Politics* 71 (2): 492-505.

Mattes, Robert, and Michael Bratton. 2007. "Learning about Democracy in Africa: Awareness, Performance, and Experience." *American Journal of Political Science* 51 (1): 192-217.

Mishler, William, and Robert Rose. 2001. "What Are the Origins of Political Trust? Testing Institutional and Cultural Theories in Post-Communist Societies." *Comparative Political* Studies 34 (1): 30-62.

Mishler, William, and Richard Rose. 2005. "What Are the Political Consequences of Trust? A Test of Cultural and Institutional Theories in Russia." *Comparative Political Studies* 38 (9): 1050-1078.

Munck ,Gerado and Jay Verkulien. 2002. "Conceptualizing and Measuring Democracy: Evaluating Alternative Indices." *Comparative Political Studies* 3(1): 5-34.

Nannestad, Peter. 2008. "What Have We Learned about Generalized Trust, if Anything?" *Annual Review of Political Science* 11: 413-436.

Nathan, Andrew James. 2003. "Authoritarian Resilience." *Journal of Democracy* 14 (1): 6-17.

Newton, Kenneth. 1997. "Social Capital and Democracy." *The American Behavioral Scientist* 40 (5): 575-586.

Newton, Kenneth. 1999. "Social and Political Trust in Established Democracies." In *Critical Citizens: Global Support for Democratic Government,* edited by Pippa Norris, 169-187. Oxford: Oxford University Press.

Newton, Kenneth. 2001. "Trust, Social Capital, Civil Society, and Democracy." *International Political Science Review* 22 (2): 201–21

Newton, Kenneth. 2006. "Political Support: Social Capital, Civil Society and Political and Economic Performance." *Political Studies* 54 (4): 846-864.

Newton, Ken, and Sonja Zmerli. 2011. "Three Forms of Trust and Their Association." *European Political Science Review* 3 (2): 169-200.

Nisbett, Richard E. 2003. *The Geography of Thought: How Asians and Westerners Think Differently...and Why*. New York: The Free Press.

Palmer, Neal A., Douglas D. Perkins and Qingwen Xu. 2011. "Social Capital and Community Participation among Migrant Workers in China." *Journal of Community Psychology* 39 (1): 89-105.

Portes, Alejandro, and Patricia Landolt. 1996. "The Downside of Social Capital." *American Prospect* 26: 18-22.

Portes, Alejandro, and Julia Sensenbrenner. 1993. "Embeddedness and Immigration: Notes on the Social Determinants of Economic Actions." *American Journal of Sociology* 98 (6): 1320-50.

Putnam, Robert D. 1995. "Tuning In and Tuning Out: The Strange Disappearance of Social Capital in America." *PS: Political Science and Politics* 28 (4): 664-683.

Putnam, Robert D., Robert Leonardi, and Raffaella Nanetti. 1993.

Making Democracy Work: Civic Transition in Modern Italy. Princeton, NJ: Princeton University Press.

Pye, Lucian W. 1992. *The Spirit of Chinese Politics.* Cambridge, MA: Harvard University Press.

Pye, Lucian W., and Mary W. Pye. 1985. *Asian Power and Politics: The Cultural Dimensions of Authority.* Cambridge, MA: Harvard University Press.

Robbins, Blaine G. 2011. "Institutional Quality and Generalized Trust: A Nonrecursive Causal Model." *Social Indicator Research* 107 (2): 235-258.

Robbins, Blaine G. 2012. "A Blessing and a Curse? Political Institutions in the Growth and Decay of Generalized Trust: A Cross-national Panel Analysis, 1980–2009." *PLoS ONE* 7 (4): 1-14.

Roßteutscher, Sigrid. 2010. "Social Capital Worldwide: Potential for Democratization or Stabilizer of Authoritarian Rule?" *American Behavioral Scientist* 53 (5): 737-757.

Secor, Anna J., and John O'Loughlin. 2005. "Social and Political Trust in Istanbul and Moscow: A Comparative Analysis of Individual and Neighborhood Effects." *Transactions of the Institute of British Geographers* 30 (1): 66-82.

Seligman, Adam B. 1997. *The Problem of Trust.* Princeton, NJ: Princeton University Press.

Seligson, Mitchell A. 2002. "The Renaissance of Political Culture or the Renaissance of the Ecological Fallacy." *Comparative Politics* 34 (3): 273-292.

Shin, Doh and Jason Wells. 2005. "Is Democracy the Only Game in Town?" *Journal of Democracy* 16 (2): 88-101.

Shin, Doh. 2012. *Confucianism and Democratization in East Asia.* New

York: Cambridge University Press.

Skocpol, Theda, and Morris P. Fiorina. 1999. *Civic Engagement in American Democracy*. New York: Russell Sage Foundation.

Steinhardt, H. Christoph. 2012. "How Is High Trust in China Possible?" Comparing the Origins of Generalized Trust in Three Chinese Societies." *Political Studies* 60 (2): 434-454.

Stolle, Dietlind. 1998. "Bowling Together, Bowling Alone: The Development of Generalized Trust in Voluntary Associations." *Political Psychology* 19 (3): 497-525.

Stolle, Dietlind, Stuart Soroka, and Richard Johnston. 2008. "When Does Diversity Erode Trust? Neighborhood Diversity, Interpersonal Trust and the Mediating Effect of Social Interactions." *Political Studies* 56 (1): 57-75.

Sztompka, Piotr. 1999. *Trust: A Sociological Theory*. Cambridge: Cambridge University Press.

Tan, Soo Jiuan, and Tambyah, Siok Kuan. 2011. "Generalized Trust and Trust in Institutions in Confucian Asia." *Social Indicator Research* 103 (3): 357-377.

Torcal, Mariano, and José Ramón Montero. 1999. "Facets of Social Capital in New Democracies." In *Social Capital and European Democracy,* edited by Jan van Deth, Marco Maraffi, Kenneth Newton, and Paul Whiteley. Oxford: Routledge.

Tu, Weiming. 1998. *Humanity and Self-cultivation: Essays in Confucian Thought.* Boston: Cheng and Tsui Company.

Uslaner, Eric M. 2002. *The Moral Foundation of Trust.* Cambridge: Cambridge University Press.

van Hoorn, Andre. 2014. "Trust Radius versus Trust Level: Radius of Trust as a Distinct Trust Construct." *American Sociological*

Review 79(6): 1256-1259.

Warren, Mark E., ed. 1999. *Democracy and Trust.* New York: Cambridge University Press.

Whiteley, Paul F. 1999. "The Origins of Social Capital." In *Social Capital and European Democracy,* edited by Jan van Deth, Marco Maraffi, Kenneth Newton, and Paul Whiteley. Routledge.

Xu, Qingwen, Douglas D. Perkins, and Julian Chun-Chung Chow. 2010. "Sense of Community, Neighboring, and Social Capital as Predictors of Local Political Participation in China." *American Journal of Community Psychology* 45: 259-271.

Yao, Xinzhong. 2000. *An Introduction to Confucianism.* New York: Cambridge University Press.

Yosano, Arinori, and Nahoko Hayashi. 2005. "Social Stratification, Intermediary Groups and Creation of Trustfulness." 理論と方法*Theory and Methods* 20 (1): 27-44.

Zakaria, Fareed. 1994. "Culture is Destiny: A Conversation with Lee Kuan Yew." *Foreign Affairs* 73 (2): 109-126.

Zmerli, Sonja, and Ken Newton. 2008. "Social Trust and Attitudes towards Democracy." *Public Opinion Quarterly* 72 (4): 706-724.

References in Chinese:

卜长莉, 2003, "'差序格局'的理论诠释及现代内涵",《社会学研究》, 第1期, 第21-29页。

BO, Changli. 2003. "Cha Xu Ge JU Theory and Its Modern Connotation," *Sociology Review* (1): 21-29.

陈占江, 2007,“差序格局与中国社会转型”,《社会科学评论》, 第3期, 第40-46页。

CHEN, Zhanjiang. 2007. “Cha Xu Ge Ju and Chinese Social Transition.” *Social Science Review* (3): 40-46.

费孝通, 2010,《乡土中国》, 上海人民出版社。

FEI, Xiaotong. 2010. *Xiang Tu Zhong Guo*. Shanghai: Shanghai People’s Press.

冯仕政, 2004,“我国当前的信任危机与社会安全”,《中国人民大学学报》, 第2期, 第25-31页。

FENG, Shizheng. 2004. “Trust Crisis and Social Security in Current China.” *Renmin University Journal of Social Science* (2): 25-31.

冯仕政, 2007,“沉默的大多数：差序格局与环境抗争”,《中国人民大学学报》, 第1期, 第122-132页。

FENG, Shizheng. 2007. “The Silent Majority: Cha Xu Ge Ju and Environmental Protest.” *Renmin University Journal of Social Science* (1): 122-132.

李伟民、梁玉成, 2002,“特殊信任与普遍信任：中国人信任的结构与特征”,《社会学研究》, 第3期, 第11-22页。

LI, Weimin, and LIANG, Yucheng. 2002. “Particular Trust and General Trust: The Structure and Features of Chinese Trust.” *Sociological Review* (3): 11-22.

龙海波, 2012.“信用政府的构建：社会资本与政府信用的关系视角”。浙江大学博士论文。

LONG, Haibo. 2012. *“Trusty Government: Social Capital and Government Credibility.”* Doctoral Dissertation of Zhengjiang University.

马戎, 2007,“‘差序格局’——中国传统社会结构和中国人行为的解读”,《社会学研究》, 第2期, 第131-142页。

MA, Rong. 2007. "Cha Xu Ge Ju: Chinese Traditional Social Structure and Chinese Behavior." *Sociological Review* (2): 131-142.

童志峰, 2006, "信任的差序格局：对乡村社会人际关系的一种解释——基于特殊主义与普遍主义信任的实证分析",《甘肃理论学刊》, 第3期, 第59-63页。

TONG, Zhifeng. 2006. "Cha Xu Ge Ju of Trust: Particular Trust and General Trust in Rural China." *Gansu Journal of Theory* (3): 59-63.

童星, 瞿华, 2010, "差序格局的结构及其制度关联性",《南京社会科学》, 第3期, 第42-48页。

TONG, Xing and QU, Hua. 2010. "The Structure of Cha Xu Ge Ju and Its Institutional Implications." *Nanjing Social Science* (3): 42-48.

王绍光、刘欣, 2002, "信任的基础：一种理性的解释",《社会学研究》, 第3期, 第23-39页。

WANG, Shaoguang, and LIU, Xin. 2002. "The Foundation of Trust: A Rational Interpretation." *Sociological Review* (3): 23-39.

亚历西斯·德·托克维尔 著, 董果良 译, 1988,《论美国的民主》, 商务印书馆。

de Tocqueville, Alexis. 1988. *Democracy in America*. Beijing: Commercial Press.

阎云翔, 2006, "差序格局与中国文化的等级观",《社会学研究》, 第4期, 第201-246页。

YAN, Yunxiang. 2006. "Cha Xu Ge Ju and Hierarchical View in Chinese Culture." *Sociological Review* (4): 201-246.

杨中芳、彭泗清, 1999, "中国人人际信任的概念化：一个人际关系的观点",《社会学研究》, 第2期, 第1-21页。

YANG, Zhongfang and PENG, Siqing. 1999. "Chinese Trust: An

Interpretation of the Concept." *Sociological Review* (2): 1-21.
杨宜音, 1999, "'自己人': 信任建构过程的个案研究", 《社会学研究》, 第2期, 第38-52页。
YANG, Yiyin. 1999. "'In-groups': A Case Study of the Construction of Trust." *Sociological Review* (2): 38-52.
翟学伟, 2009, "再论'差序格局'的贡献、局限于理论遗产", 《中国社会科学》, 第3期, 第152-158页。
ZHAI, Xuewei. 2009. "Re-discuss the Contribution, Limitation and Theoretical Heritage of 'Cha Xu Ge Ju' Theory." *Chinese Journal of Social Science* (3): 152-158.

7

Appraising the Quality of Government in South Korea: Exploratory Application of a Multidimensional Model

Youngho Cho

Sogang University, South Korea

Introduction

The study of quality of government or good government is a fast-growing industry among disciplines such as political science, economics, and developmental studies. Given that social science of the 1970s–1980s, after the behavioral revolution, had focused on empirical and scientific research for the purpose of using available data and testing theories and, thus, had neglected normative and classical questions such as what is good government and how should government rule, these studies are an academic and important attempt to solve real political problems (Fukuyama 2014; Putnam 1993).

Since the 1990s, international organizations and academic scholars alike have attempted to evaluate institutions, performance, and quality of governance and government, although they have not agreed upon the term *good government*. For representative examples, consider Transparency International, which has published the Corruption Perceptions Index (CPI) since 1995, annually ranking countries by expert and mass surveys, and the World Bank, which has applied a multidimensional model to evaluate the quality of various aspects of governance. In academic society, Bo Rothstein and his colleagues at the University of Gothenburg, Sweden, have identified the core principle of good government as impartiality and have measured qualities of national as well as local governments in Europe (Charron, Dijkstra, and Lapuente 2015; Holmberg, Rothstein, and Nasiritousi 2009; Rothstein 2011). In South Korea, several scholars have critically introduced recent literature on good government, and some of them have presented empirical results (Kim 2011; Lee 2013; Park and Chang 2012).

Why has the literature of good government been increasing in both advanced and developing countries? Three underlying conditions pertain to this academic and practical focus. First of all, public trust and satisfaction with government have declined in advanced and developing countries. Given that money and capital run an economy, government trust is a political resource that ensures government and politics work together. Accordingly, the decline of political trust leads to the political decay of a government's problem-solving capacity. Scholarly studies on good government are a natural response to this phenomenon (Pharr and Putnam 2000).

The second condition is that the global waves of democratization since 1974 have not substantially improved socioeconomic development and government qualities (Carothers 2002; Charron and Lapuente 2010; O'Donnell, Vargas, Iazzatta, and Cullel 2004). Whereas scholars of comparative politics in the 1980s–1990s implicitly expected that democratization would contribute to socioeconomic and political development, recent scholars reached consensus that the four decades of democratization around the world have turned out to be limited (Fukuyama 2015). Overall, the introduction of democratic institutions such as multiparty competition and elections is a necessary condition, rather than a sufficient one, for good government, and, therefore, a direct approach is needed to investigate the nature, causes, and consequence of good government.

The final underlying condition is directly related to state collapse and government failure in the underdeveloped world (Bates 2008; Fukuyama 2014; Rotberg 2003). Since the end of the Cold War, as the United States and the Soviet Union have stopped various supports for weak states in Africa, the Middle East, and Asia and the low price of the primary commodities has led to economic recession in these states, government failure and state collapse have emerged as a puzzling international issue. Genocide, refugees, civil wars, and terrorism have centered in these weak or failed states. Naturally, theoretical scholars raise questions about state-building and government reconstruction, and empirical scholars attempt to answer such fundamental questions as what is good government, how is government reconstructed, and how can its qualities be enhanced.

Recent studies on the quality of government are twofold. A majority of studies have focused on the social, economic, political, and cultural consequences of specific qualities of government. However, there are a lack of studies on what good government is, how it can be measured, and what it originated from. This study is an attempt to contribute to the second issue and responds to two specific problems of prior studies. In conceptualizing and measuring the quality of government, some studies adopt a minimalist approach to expand comparability across countries, but their narrow conception of good government does not cover the multifaceted attributes of modern government in advanced and developing countries. Other studies relying on governance propose a multidimensional framework, but their model evaluates both societal and governmental characteristics as well as their interactions. As a result, the multidimensional framework has limited validity and reliability in accurately capturing the quality of government.

This study is premised on the assumption that evaluation of good government lies in citizens' collective judgment. If public evaluation of governmental quality is low, that is important evidence that government is not functioning well. By the same token, if citizens positively evaluate specific domains of government, this suggests that its quality is high at least in those domains. Therefore, the quality of democracy is assessed from the perspectives of mass citizens who experience its practices on a daily basis.

Analyzing results of a nationwide survey, this study shows that a majority of Koreans evaluate their government's quality as problematic and evaluate procedural quality more negatively than outcome quality. This assessment reflects their experience of authoritarian modernization and flawed democracy after democratization. These findings indicate that Korean government needs to improve procedural quality rather than outcome quality.

This chapter is organized into five sections. The first section reviews earlier works on the quality of government. The second introduces the new framework for assessing governmental quality in Korea. The third offers citizen assessments of general and specific qualities of government. The final section summarizes the new framework proposed and tested herein and highlights my survey research findings.

Prior Research

The quality of democracy has become a subject of increasing and widespread concern in policy circles and the scholarly community (Fukuyama 2014; Putnam 1993; Rothstein 2011). What is good government in the modern era? How well do governments respond to various public demands? What particular quality or qualities of government are most lacking in advanced and developing countries? What efforts are needed to improve governmental qualities? These questions have been raised in response to a growing sense of public discontent with government and state failure. To answer these questions, a group of scholars have adopted a minimalist approach by relying on a single attribute of modern government, but another group have focused on a maximalist one by highlighting several characteristics.

The recent resurgence of academic interest on good government started with Robert Putnam's (1993) monumental study on the quality of Italian regional governments during the 1970s and 1980s. In his famous book, *Making Democracy Work*, Putnam evaluated the quality of local representative governments and examined the historical and cultural origins of good and bad governments. According to him, a good democratic government not only considers the demands of its citizenry (that is, it is responsive) but also acts efficaciously upon these demands (that is, it is effective)" (63). Thus, Putnam defined the quality of government as responsiveness and effectiveness and evaluated the quality of Italian local governments using twelve indicators of the three domains: policy processes, policy pronouncements, and policy implementation. As Putnam stated (63), his concept of good government was based on Robert Dahl's theory of democracy. In his book, *Polyarchy*, Dahl held that "a key characteristic of a democracy is the continuing responsiveness of the government to the preferences of its citizens, considered as political equals" (1973, 1). Putnam applied a single attribute of democracy to operationalize good government, and his study focused on the democratic quality of good government. In his framework, bad government definitely lacked democratic responsiveness.

Since Putnam's founding study, a group of scholars in the Quality of Government (QoG) Institute at University of Gothenburg have presented innovative studies within the minimalist approach. Under the direction of Bo Rothstein, scholars at this institute have defined the core quality of good government as impartiality and have documented empirical assessments of the quality of national and local governments in Europe. In particular, this institute has measured the degree to which national governments around the world are impartial in dealing with public demands using expert surveys. According to Rothstein, *impartiality* means that "when implementing laws and policies, government officials shall not take into consideration anything but the citizen/case that is not stipulated beforehand in the policy or the law" (2011, 13). Rothstein agrees with Putnam that the quality of government should be assessed on the basis of the output side, rather than the input side, of the Eastonian political system. However, his model is more procedural than that of Putnam in the sense that the former emphasizes how impartial public officials are in handling citizens' demand and enforcing policies and laws. In particular, Rothstein and his colleagues have empirically measured the quality of government by focusing on three dimensions: quality, impartiality, and corruption in public services such as education, health care, and law enforcement (Charron, Dijkstra, and Lapuente 2015; Holmberg and Rothstein 2014; Rothstein 2011).

The strength of these minimalist models stressing responsiveness or impartiality is that they enable a comparative analysis of cross-national and cross-regional governments due to their simplicity. Indeed, Putnam compared twenty regional governments of Italy, and the QoG Institute examined qualities of 212 local governments in Europe and 135 national governments around the world.

This comparative utility notwithstanding, one critical weakness of these minimalist models is that they do not capture the diversity and complexity of modern governments around the world. Because they focus on a single attribute, they not only are unable to assess other desirable attributes of good government but also fail to offer practical implications for other domains. In particular, democratic responsiveness and impartiality lose analytical utility when studying countries in which state institutions collapse and governments fail to provide public safety. As Huntington (1968) aptly pointed out, the fundamental goods of government are order and safety. In countries that lack order and safety, if someone applies responsiveness and impartiality, the assessment would be limited and its policy suggestions might signal a wrong direction. In response to this limitation, Fukuyama (2013) proposes another minimalist model and argues that quality of a government depends on its capacity to maintain rules and order.

Fukuyama's model expands a comparative scope to cover both modern and premodern governments, but it naturally excludes other desirable attributes of good government in the modern era.

Overall, modern good government is a multidimensional phenomena comprising its necessary and desirable attributes.

To overcome this intrinsic limitation of minimalist models, international organizations have proposed multidimensional models and assess the quality of government. Although these organizations prefer the term *governance* to *government*, the terms are used interchangeably in academic studies because the organizations weight down with activities of public administration. The World Bank is a leading institution in this field. Since 1995, the World Bank has annually ranked countries by six governance indicators: 1) Voice and Accountability; 2) Political Stability and Absence of Violence; 3) Government Effectiveness; 4) Regulatory Quality; 5) Rule of Law; and 6) Control of Corruption (Kaufmann, Kraay, and Mastruzzi 2009). Since 2008, the Bertelsmann Foundation has also documented the quality of sustainable governance among the OECD countries and examined policy performance, democracy, and governance.

In academic circles, Fukuyama (2014) and Agnafors (2013) have proposed a multidimensional model of assessing good government. In his recent magnum opus, Fukuyama contends that good government in the modern period needs three attributes in balance: functioning state institutions, democratic accountability, and rule of law. Using this framework, Fukuyama traces a historical trajectory of how the governments of the United States, Germany, Italy, and Greece have experienced political decay and development (ch. 13). Taking a conceptual approach, Agnafors critically reviews prior social science frameworks and proposes a new framework with an emphasis on an ethical dimension. According to him, good government should meet seven criteria: public ethos, good decision making, reason giving, principle of beneficence, rule of law, efficiency, and stability.

Unlike the minimalist approaches, multidimensional models have a ability to assess the quality of government in a comprehensive way. However, existing multidimensional models capture attributes of society and government as well as their interactions. For example, rule of law in the models of the World Bank and Fukuyama reflects social and historical traditions of law in addition to the law-abidingness of public officials and judicial independence. Due to this partial validity problem, scholars have selectively used available indicators from the World Bank and other international organizations. For example, Norris (2012) employed just five world governance indicators, excluding voice and accountability, and Charron and his colleagues (2013, 2015) included four indicators, dropping voice and accountability as well as political stability and absence of violence. Moreover, Holmberg and his colleagues (2009) combined government effectiveness and rule of law from the World Bank and the CPI from Transparency International. As a consequence, existing multidimensional models are limited in narrowing their measuring target down government, and therefore, they suffer from partial validity and reliability (Agnafors 2013; Kurtz and Schrank 2007). Finally, the theoretical models of Fukuyama and Agnafors have not yet led to empirical and quantitative indicators.

In summary, since the 1990s, both scholars and international organizations have made an increasing effort to evaluate the quality of government. One group prefers a unidimensional model of evaluating governmental quality, but another advocates a multidimensional one. The former has difficulty in addressing the complex nature of modern government, and the latter has a problem with validity and reliability. Moreover, as Agnafors (2013, 434) stated, prior studies have proposed empirical frameworks, but they have not justified them well. These problems have resulted in existing models failing to provide practical suggestions on what is needed to improve the quality of government in developing countries (Grindle 2007; Weiss 2000). In response to these problems, this study seeks to provide a new model of assessing the quality of government and applies that model to the case of South Korea.

Good Government in the Modern Era

This study assumes that the quality of political institutions and organizations is by nature multidimensional and tends to vary across historical phases. In particular, desirable attributes of good government differ between the modern and premodern eras, although necessary and universal elements of good government such as political order originated from the premodern era. Moreover, although the menu of necessary attributes of good government does not vary between the modern and premodern eras, their contents are not the same. For example, political order and safety were maintained collectively by kings, churches, and local lords in the medieval period, but they are provided by government monopolizing coercive violence methods in this present era.

In addition, this study does not agree with the relativism of Andrews (2010), who states that meanings of good government vary so much across different countries that it is almost impossible to establish a universal model of appraising good government. Modern government, which originated in France and England of the seventeenth and eighteenth centuries, had been exported to Central and Eastern Europe in the nineteenth century, and non-Western countries have rushed to imitate the Western style of modern government in the twentieth century. Moreover, waves of globalization, democratization, and independence have increased modern forms of government in every corner of the world and promoted their convergence in the developing and advanced countries. Although Europe has experimented with a supranational organization, the European Union, and government failure has frequently occurred in Africa, there is consensus among a majority of scholars that modern states would be a dominant trend in the twenty-first century. Because this notion is widely accepted, scholars and international organizations define modern states as units of analysis and compare countries by government performance, economic prosperity, and societal characteristics.

With this premise, I argue that the quality of modern government consists of several necessary and desirable attributes that have been recognized by theorists and empirical scholars since the beginning of the modern era. Both historically and theoretically, many attributes have been proposed and advocated, but some of them have become marginalized and lost their vitality as a necessary component of good government. The general process of making one attribute a necessary principle of modern government goes like this: A small group of scholars and elites propose ideas, the ideas struggle against alternative concepts, and finally, some of them survive to become necessary attributes that drive government reforms (Berman 2006; Diamond 2008; Fukuyama 2014; Huntington 1991). Once a certain idea is politically recognized as a core component of modern government, it tends to take on a life of its own and create its own tradition within the political sphere. Some political attributes recognized as necessary and desirable in modern government have been specified and realized during the process of state-building and its subsquent reforms in the Western world. These attributes have then been exported to non-Western countries, thereby facilitating globalization of modern government in this present era (Anderson 1991; Scott 1999; Tilly 1992).

This study pays attention to five attributes as necessary and desirable components of modern good government. These are security, rule of law, justice, democratic accountability, and welfare;

they have been established as core norms of modern and advanced government during the historical process of state-building, state expansion, and state reform. These attributes have been proposed by political thinkers and elites and recognized as governing principles of modern government as a result of a series of political struggles in modern history. Although episodes associated with each attribute vary across different countries and historical phases, they are widely regarded as necessary and desirable components of advanced modern government.

First of all, security (internal and external) and rule of law were advocated by early liberalists and have been accepted as sine qua non purposes of modern government. As both Hobbes ([1651] 1982) and Huntington (1968) emphasized, the fundamental function of government and state is to provide political order and safety at the domestic level and protect people from foreign threats. The modern concept of internal and external security is different from that of the premodern times. As based on rational authority, modern government monopolizes coercive methods and protects citizens' properties and lives. However, premodern governments relied for their authority upon traditions, God, and nature, and they did not control coercive violence measures. Similar differences exist regarding rule of law. The modern concept of rule of law indicates that use of government power must abide by rational contracts between rulers and people, which are stipulated as laws. On the other hand, rule of law during the medieval period was influenced by the German customary law and advanced through the Investiture

Controversy between church and secular kings (Fukuyama 2011; Tamanaha 2004). Moreover, modern rule of law over government activities was developed by early liberalists and the bourgeoisie class to advocate limited government and civil liberties such as freedom of religion, expression, and economic activities.

The next attributes, justice and democratic accountability, were raised by liberalists and democrats of the nineteenth and early twentieth centuries and have been accepted as core principles of modern government. Unlike early liberal thinkers, liberal democrats of the late nineteenth century argued that government must uphold justice and equality, treat its citizens as politically equal, and, thus, various forms of discrimination against women, workers, and slaves should be abolished. Justice has two types, procedural and distributional. *Procedural justice* requires that government consider citizens and groups in an equal and impartial way when it prepares and enforces policies. *Distributional justice* means that tax and duties for state should be fairly imposed. In premodern times, justice was limited because political rights were given only to certain families, groups, and classes. It was also discriminative because differential duties and tax were common. On the other hand, justice is a core principle of modern government in that governmental burdens should be fairly distributed and people are equal before government and laws.

Democratic accountability is used as an attribute of government in this study, rather than democratic procedures such as elections, mass participation, and multiparty competition. I agree with prior scholars that democratic quality of government lies on the output side of political system rather than the input side (Putnam 1993; Rothstein 2011). Therefore, this study is concerned with the substantive quality of democracy, rather than the procedural quality, that government produces. Democratic accountability in the activities of government can be judged by two dimensions. One is how much government responds to citizens' demands. Another is how loyal public officials are to their principal of people. The second dimension can be reversely measured by how much governmental officials betray public interests and pursue their own interests, which is a standard definition of *corruption*. These substantial ideals of democracy have become necessary criteria that international organizations and scholars use to evaluate the performance and integrity of government (Diamond and Morlino 2004).

Finally, welfare was advocated by social democrats and progressive liberals and has been recognized as a necessary attribute of good government in the modern era (Berman 2006; Marshall 1950). Although Esping-Anderson (1990) identified three types of welfare states in the Western world, governments of advanced countries provide more welfare benefits than those of developing countries do. In the non-Western world, Singapore supplies a public housing system, Japan has a public health care system, and China maintains the largest decommodified proportion of a national economy. Nonetheless, high and wide welfare policies of the Western governments are regarded as a desirable and necessary component of modern advanced government among ordinary people and scholars alike.

This study does not claim that the multidimensional model comprising the five attributes is a comprehensive and exclusive framework, given that the modern state is huge in size and population and the modern government responds to various interests, values, and principles of citizens and groups. Some interests, values, and principles are in conflict rather than harmony, and modern government is a product of political struggle, formation, and reformation. Moreover, globalization has promoted convergence of modern governments in appearance as well as divergence of their practices through increased communication and imitation. Nonetheless, the five components (security, rule of law, justice, democratic accountability, and welfare) have been established as necessary attributes of modern government in advanced countries, and they drive government reforms as desirable principles in developing countries.

Furthermore, the framework elaborated herein will overcome the limitation of minimalist models and improve partial validity and reliability by focusing on government and covering its various dimensions. South Korea is a prototypical case with which to study good government in the non-Western developing nations because the country has experienced successful state-building and peaceful democratization. Finally, this study analyzing public opinion survey will provide information about what aspects of Korean government are negatively or positively evaluated and what kinds of reform are needed.

Empirical Results

How do ordinary Koreans evaluate the quality of their government? What aspects does the Korean government need to improve to become a good government? What structure underlies Koreans' thinking about their government? To answer these question, this study uses the public opinion data culled from the Good Government Survey of Sogang Institute of Political Studies (SIPS) during the months of October and December 2015. The SIPS conducted personal interviews with a randomly chosen national sample of 1,501 Korean citizens to tap their opinions about various aspects of Korean government. Whereas an expert survey has potential sampling bias, a nationwide face-to-face survey has been widely adopted as a valid and representative method for evaluating the quality of government (Charron, Dijkstra, and Lapuente 2015; Putnam 1993; Rothstein 2011).

To evaluate the quality of Korean government in the five domains, this study employed a set of two questions for each domain, for a total of ten. The questions are designed to clarify evaluation objects as governmental activities and outputs. As a result, government or public officials were specified in eight of the ten questions and respondents would be aware in the other two questions that government is a service provider. Respondents were allowed to choose one of four Likert-scale answers, from the most negative to the most positive.

Table 1. Measurements for Evaluation of Good Government

Dimension	Subdimension	Question
Security	External Security	How well or poorly does our government respond to foreign threats including North Korea?
	Internal Security	How safe would you say our country is?
Rule of Law	Law-abidingness	How well do you think public officials abide by laws?
	Control of Power Abuse	How much do you agree or disagree with the following statement? Our government tends to abuse its authority.
Justice	Procedural Justice	How much do you agree or disagree with the following statement? Our government impartially considers stakeholders and related groups when deciding policies.
	Distributional Justice	How much do you agree or disagree with the following statement? Our government fairly imposes taxes or military duties on all citizens.

Democratic Accountability	Responsiveness	How much do you agree or disagree with the following statement? Our government importantly reflects public opinion in the policy-making process.
	Anti-corruption	How corrupt or clean do you think our public officials are?
Welfare	Welfare Level	What do you think about the overall level of welfare in our country?
	Welfare Effectiveness	How much do you agree or disagree with the following statement? Welfare benefits are appropriately delivered to those in need.

Source: Sogang Institute of Political Studies 2015 Good Government Survey.

Table 1 shows measurements and questions employed in this study. First of all, to measure the quality of the Korean government in the security dimension, I used how well or poorly their government responds to foreign threats including North Korea (external security) and how safe their country is (internal security). Next, how well public officials abide by laws and whether their government abuses its authority are used to measure the rule of law dimension of governmental quality. Third, whether their government impartially considers stakeholders and related groups when deciding policies and whether their government fairly imposes tax or military duties on all citizens are respectively assigned to examine procedural and procedural justice. Fourth, responsiveness and anticorruption, facets of the democratic accountability dimension, elicit two questions: how much their government reflects public opinion into the policy-making process and how corrupt or clear public officials are. Finally, in the welfare dimension, the general level of welfare is assessed by what they think about the level of welfare in the country, and welfare effectiveness is measured by whether welfare benefits are appropriately delivered to those in need. These two questions of the welfare dimension are standard measures of welfare attitudes.

What dimensions are most positively or negatively assessed in the eyes of ordinary Korean citizens? What proportion of Korean citizens are satisfied with each of the ten subdimensions? Table 2 reports how Korean citizens evaluate each of the ten subdimensions of the quality of government. Generally, there are three dimensions about which Koreans made a positive assessment: external security, internal security, and level of welfare. In the security dimension, a majority of Korean citizens think their government protects the country from external threats such as North Korea and public safety is not a concern. This finding is understandable because South Korea had three years of war against North Korea during the 1950s and has had a cold war for more than a half century. During the state-building period of the 1970s and 1980s under the dictatorial leadership of military generals Chung-hee Park and Doo-hwan Chun, the Korean government empowered coercive agencies such as the military, the police, the Central Intelligence Agency, and other related organizations. Moreover, although North Korea's state capacity was stronger than that of South Korea before the early 1970s, the South Korean economy has continuously grown and North Korea has failed to compete against South Korea without such special methods as nuclear weapons. Since North Korea has disappeared as a fatal threat from public sentiment, six of ten South Koreans evaluate national security as positive. By the mirror effect, 56% of the respondents think South Korea is generally safe.

Table 2. Public Evaluation of the Quality of Korean Government

Dimension	Subdimension	Positive	Negative	Score (1–4)
Security	External Security	60.2%	39.8%	2.62
	Internal Security	56.4	43.6	2.57
Rule of Law	Law-abidingness	30.4	69.6	2.27
	Control of Power Abuse	25.1	74.9	2.11
Justice	Procedural Justice	34.0	66.0	2.29
	Distributional Justice	36.1	63.9	2.25
Democratic Accountability	Responsiveness	35.1	64.9	2.27
	Anticorruption	17.4	82.6	2.00
Welfare	Welfare Level	46.0	54.0	2.46
	Welfare Effectiveness	35.9	64.1	2.29

Source: Sogang Institute of Political Studies 2015 Good Government Survey.

As with the security dimension, the welfare dimension is positively assessed by Koreans. However, there is a small gap between the general level of welfare and its effectiveness. About 46% agree that the general level of welfare in South Korea is high or very high. On the other hand, 54% think it is low or very low. Because half of Korean citizens consider the current level of welfare to be sufficient, this result suggests that welfare expansion would be very difficult in this country. However, with regard to welfare effectiveness, about two thirds of the respondents think that welfare benefits are not distributed to those in need. This means that ordinary citizens support welfare reforms within the limited scope of government spending rather than welfare expansion. Given that South Korea was the poorest country in the world during the period of the 1950s–1970s, old generations tend to think that the current welfare programs are acceptable.

When it comes to the other three dimensions, only a minority of Koreans gave a positive evaluation. Among the six specific subdimensions, only 17% and 25% think that public officials are clean and their government does not abuse its authority, respectively. On the flip side, 83% and 75% state their government is corrupt and overuses its power, respectively. Moreover, about 70% of the respondents judge that public officials do not respect and abide by laws. About two thirds of Koreans assess that procedural and distributional justice and democratic responsiveness do not hold in their country. They think that public officials partially favor some over others and that government burdens such as tax and military duties are not fairly imposed. They also estimate that their government does not reflect public opinion in its policies. From these results, it is not clear which group the Korean government favors or discriminates against, in the eyes of ordinary citizens. However, it is clear that South Korea's strong government is impartial in managing citizens' affairs and considers their opinions in the policy-making process. Considering the fact that Korean economic and social development has been directed by state plans, these results imply that there is a significant gap between what and how government produces its outcomes and what people expect and demand.

If I rank the ten subdimensions by public evaluation score, corruption is the most serious concern among Korean citizens (2.00). Power abuse is ranked as the next lowest (2.11). Five subdimensions constitute the moderate group with scores of 2.25–2.29: distributional justice (2.25), democratic responsiveness (2.27), law-abidingness (2.27), procedural justice (2.29), and welfare effectiveness (2.29). Finally, external security (2.62), internal security (2.57), and welfare level (2.46) form a group receiving relatively positive assessments.

What structural domains exist within the public evaluation of the ten subdimensions in the quality of Korean government? Does the public valuation have one underlying factor or a few? To answer these questions, this study conducted a factor analysis. According to Table 3, the Kaiser-Meyer-Olkin measure (0.845) and Bartlett's test of sphericity suggest that the factor analysis satisfy a minimal standard and the result would be valid and reliable. Underlying the Koreans' evaluation of governmental quality, two latent factors were found: procedural and outcome. Given that security and welfare are substantial outputs of government and the other three belong to the governmental process of dealing with public affairs and treating citizens, this result indicates that Korean citizens are able to distinguish government process from its outcome.

Table 3. Factor Analysis: Structure of Koreans' Evaluation of Governmental Quality

Dimension	Subdimension	Process Factor	Outcome Factor
Security	External Security		.483
	Internal Security		.473
Rule of Law	Law-abidingness	.386	
	Control of Power Abuse	.395	
Justice	Procedural Justice	.608	
	Distributional Justice	.631	
Democratic Accountability	Responsiveness	.599	
	Anticorruption	.384	
Welfare	Welfare Level		.593
	Welfare Effectiveness		.523

Note: Extraction method: principal axis factoring. Rotation method: varimax with Kaiser normalization. Kaiser-Meyer-Olkin measure: 0.845. Bartlett's test of sphericity: significance level ≤ 0.00.

What does this result mean about the quality of Korean government? The factor analysis shows that Korean citizens are more negative about the government's process than its substantial outcome. Considering that a majority of citizens consider internal and external security as good and nearly half of them assess the general level of welfare as high, the Korean government is not negatively regarded about what it produces. On the other hand, a majority of Koreans appear to be dissatisfied with how government addresses policies and treats citizens and organizations. This is obviously related to state-directed development over the last five decades. The Korean government had planned socioeconomic development under the direction of military dictators during the 1970s and 1980s, and its citizens and social organizations were forcefully mobilized to follow those plans. Ten years after the democratic transition of 1987, Korea faced the Asian financial crisis and accepted an International Monetary Fund (IMF) austerity policy in 1997. Even during this period of restructuring, economic reforms were driven by the government. From these developmental experiences, ordinary citizens still view the Korean government as goal-oriented rather than process-oriented.

The empirical results presented in this study indicate that the Korean government needs to improve its process of making policies and treating citizens. Developmental government during the military dictatorship attempted to exclude citizens' participation in the policy-making process. According to the analysis, even democratically elected administrations since 1987 have not fully upheld such principles as justice, rule of law, and democratic accountability. In particular, political leaders have often been involved in political corruption scandals, have represented regional interests, and have relied on informal and clandestine political rules, rather than formal and transparent ones, to implement major national policies. According to World Governance Indicators measured by the World Bank, in two domains—rule of law and control of corruption—South Korea has shown little progress since the Kim Young Sam government (Choi 2011; Im 2011). These problems among political and bureaucratic officials hinder the Korean government from becoming a good government. Moreover, reforms of government process will be a key solution to declining political trust among Korean citizens (Tyler 2006)

Conclusion

A consensus has emerged among scholars of political science, public administration, economics, and developmental studies that the quality of government should be improved to lead economic development and social advancement. This consensus is a natural response to increasing public discontent with government in advanced countries and government failure in underdeveloped ones. Following this consensus and concern, scholars and international organizations alike have assessed various aspects of modern government such as quality, performance, and nature. Building on this effort, the case study analyzing how Korean citizens evaluate the quality of government has made three contributions.

First of all, existing frameworks for evaluating the quality government have presented conceptual and empirical problems despite their strengths and utilities. In particular, minimalist models are not able to cover the complexity of modern government, and multidimensional approaches are too broad to focus on governmental activities and outputs. To compensate for this problem, this study proposed a new multidimensional model of assessing the quality of government. With the premise that modern government first emerged in Western Europe, spread to non-Western countries, and waves of globalization have driven the appearance of modern governments around the world, the study defined five necessary and desirable attributes of good government: security, rule of law, justice, democratic accountability, and welfare.

Next, I applied this framework to the case of South Korea, which sequentially experienced state-building and democracy-building. Analyzing a nationwide public opinion survey, this research found that ordinary Korean citizens are able to assess the quality of government in a balanced manner. The results suggest that Koreans evaluate the security and welfare dimensions as moderate but the other three as negative. Thus, it is reasonable to conclude that the general quality of Korean government is low: in the eyes of Korean citizens, the specific qualities in the security and welfare dimensions are medium and those in rule of law, justice, and democratic accountability dimensions are low.

Furthermore, this study found that there are two underlying structures behind what Korean think about the quality of government. The five dimensions are grouped into process and outcome factors. The process factor includes rule of law, justice, and democratic accountability; the outcome factor comprises security and welfare. This result indicates that Korean citizens distinguish between government activities (how government deals with citizens and their demands) and outputs (what government produces). More important, the quality of government in the process domain is lower than that of the outcome domain. This result leads to a policy implication that Korean government needs to improve its process quality.

Why do Koreans think that the quality of government is low in its process domain? Although this study has not attempted to investigate causes of this phenomena, it appears that state-directed development and reform of South Korea have been consequentially productive but have a dark side. That is, a majority of Korean people think that government officials do not respect rule of law but are corrupt and that government benefits and burdens are not fairly distributed. Clearly, government distrust seems to grow from this process. Moreover, the findings presented in this study confirm that the democratic experiment of the last three decades has failed to make Korean government impartial, law-abiding, clean, and fair.

All in all, South Korea has made an effort to stabilize democratic institutions such as multiparty competition and elections, but the effect of such democratization at the regime level is limited in the sphere of government.

Finally, this chapter has broadened the comparative scope of studying good government. Whereas prior studies have heavily focused on Europe and advanced countries, this study has examined good government in a country in the non-Western and developing world: South Korea. South Korea has a strong state tradition and has experienced both strong state-building and peaceful democracy-building in its modern history. Nonetheless, the country has not ended the Korean War against North Korea, democratic quality is low, and welfare programs are shallow. In this sense, existing models of good government are limited in their application to developing countries. As a result, I suggest that the security and welfare dimensions should be included in multidimensional models of evaluating the quality of government in developing countries.

References

Agnafors, Marcus. 2013. "Quality of Government: Toward a More Complex Definition." *American Political Science Review* 107 (3): 433-45.

Anderson, Benedict. 1991. *Imagined Communities: Reflections on the Origin and Spread of Nationalism*. New York: Verso.

Andrews, Matt. 2010. "Good Government Means Different Things in Different Countries." *Governance* 23 (1): 7-35.

Bates, Robert H. 2008. "State Failure." *Annual Review of Political Science* 11 (1): 1-12.

Berman, Sheri. 2006. *The Primacy of Politics: Social Democracy and the Making of Europe's Twentieth Century*. New York: Cambridge University Press.

Bertelsmann Foundation. 2014. "Methodology of Sustainable Governance Index." Güterslo, Germany: Bertelsmann Stiftung.

Carothers, Thomas. 2002. "The End of the Transition Paradigm." *Journal of Democracy* 13 (1): 5-21.

Charron, Nicholas, Lewis Dijkstra, and Victor Lapuente. 2015. "Mapping the Regional Divide in Europe: A Measure for Assessing Quality of Government in 206 European Regions." *Social Indicators Research* 122 (2): 315-46.

Charron, Nicholas, and Victor Lapuente. 2010. "Does Democracy Produce Quality of Government?" *European Journal of Political Research* 49 (4): 443-70.

———. 2013. "Why Do Some Regions in Europe Have a Higher Quality of Government?" *Journal of Politics* 75 (3): 567-82.

Choi, Jang-Jip. 2012. *Democracy after Democratization: The Korean Experience*. Stanford: Shorenstein Asia-Pacific Research Center.

Dahl, Robert A. 1971. *Polyarchy: Participation and Opposition.* New Haven, CT: Yale University Press

Diamond, Larry. 2008. *The Spirit of Democracy: The Struggle to Build Free Societies throughout the World.* New York: Times Books.

Diamond, Larry, and Leonardo Morlino. 2005. *Assessing the Quality of Democracy*. Baltimore: Johns Hopkins University Press.

Esping-Andersen, Gøsta. 1990. *The Three Worlds of Welfare Capitalism.* Princeton, NJ: Princeton University Press.

Fukuyama, Francis. 2011. *The Origins of Political Order: From Prehuman Times to the French Revolution.* New York: Farrar, Straus and Giroux.

———. 2013. "What Is Governance?" *Governance* 26 (3): 347-68.

———. 2014. *Political Order and Political Decay: From the Industrial Revolution to the Globalization of Democracy*. New York: Farrar, Straus and Giroux.

———. 2015. "Why Is Democracy Performing So Poorly?" *Journal of Democracy* 26 (1): 11-20.

Grindle, Merilee S. 2007. "Good Enough Governance Revisited." *Development Policy Review* 25 (5): 553-74.

Hobbes, Thomas. (1651) 1982. *Leviathan.* New York: Penguin Classics.

Holmberg, Soren, and Bo Rothstein. 2014. *Good Government: The Relevance of Political Science.* Northampton, MA: Edward Elgar.

Holmberg, Sören, Bo Rothstein, and Naghmeh Nasiritousi. 2009. "Quality of Government: What You Get." *Annual Review of Political Science* 12 (1): 135-61.

Huntington, Samuel P. 1968. *Political Order in Changing Societies*. New Haven, CT: Yale University Press.

Huntington, Samuel P. 1991. *The Third Wave: Democratization in the Late Twentieth Century*. Norman: University of Oklahoma Press

Im, Hyug Baeg. 2011. "Better Democracy, Better Economic Growth? South Korea." *International Political Science Review* 32 (5): 579-98.

Kaufmann, Daniel, Aart Kraay, and Massimo Mastruzzi. 2009. "Governance Matters 2009: Learning from over a Decade of the Worldwide Governance Indicators." Washington, DC: World Bank.

Kim, Sunhyuk. "Quality of Government and Civil Society: A Critical Review of the Existing Literature and an Exploration into New Measures." *Journal of Governmental Studies* 17 (3): 49-79.

Lee, Hyeon-Woo. 2013. "Quality of Government: Critical Review of Impartiality." *Korean Journal of Area Studies*. 31 (1): 7-28.

Marshall, T. H. 1950. *Citizenship and Social Class: Other Essays*. London: Cambridge University Press.

Norris, Pippa. 2012 . *Making Democratic Governance Work: The Impact of Regimes on Prosperity, Welfare and Peace*. New York: Cambridge University Press.

O'Donnell, Guillermo, Jorge Vargas Cullell, Osvaldo M. Iazzetta, and Jorge Vargas Cullel 2004. *The Quality of Democracy: Theory and Applications*. South Bend, IN: University of Notre Dame Press.

Park, Chong-Min, and Yongjin Chang. 2012. "Good Citizens and Good Government." *Journal of Governmental Studies* 18 (1): 3-22.

Pharr, Susan J., and Robert D. Putnam. 2000. *Disaffected Democracies:*

What's Troubling the Trilateral Democracies. Princeton, NJ: Princeton University Press.

Putnam, Robert D. 1993. *Making Democracy Work: Civic Traditions in Modern Italy* Princeton, NJ: Princeton University Press.

Rotberg, Robert I. 2003. *When States Fail: Causes and Consequences*. Princeton, NJ: Princeton University Press.

Rothstein, Bo. 2011. *The Quality of Government: Corruption, Social Trust, and Inequality in International Perspective*. Chicago: University of Chicago Press.

Scott, James. 1999. *Seeing Like a State: How Certain Schemes to Improve the Human Condition Have Failed*. New Haven, CT: Yale University Press

Tamanaha, Brian Z. 2004. *On the Rule of Law: History, Politics, and Theory*. Cambridge, MA: Wiley-Blackwell.

Tilly, Charles. 1992. *Coercion, Capital and European States: AD 990–1992*. Cambridge, MA: Wiley-Blackwell.

Transparency International. 2015. "Corruption Perceptions Index 2015." Berlin, Germany: Transparency International.

Tyler, Tom R. 2006. *Why People Obey the Law*. Princeton,NJ: Princeton University Press.

Weiss, Thomas G. 2000. "Governance, Good Governance and Global Governance: Conceptual and Actual Challenges." *Third World Quarterly* 21 (5): 795-814.

List of Contributors

Benny Teh Cheng Guan is Senior Lecturer at the School of Social Sciences, Universiti Sains Malaysia in Penang, Malaysia. His research interests include East Asian regionalism, human security, ASEAN community building, traditional security cooperation and good governance. He is the editor of Foreign Policy and Security in an Asian Century: Threats, Strategies and Policy Choices (World Scientific, 2014) and Human Security: Securing East Asia's Future (Springer, 2012).

Youngho Cho is an assistant professor in political science at Sogang University, Seoul, South Korea. He earned his doctoral degree in political science from the University of Missouri-Columbia. His research includes public attitudes about democracy and government. His papers have appeared in Political Studies, Democratization, and Political Research Quarterly.

Willy Jou is Associate Professor at Waseda University in Japan. He received a PhD in political science from the University of California, Irvine. His research topics include public opinion, party systems and ideology. He has published in Asian Survey, British Journal of Political Science, Communist and Post-Communist Studies, International Political Science Review,

Journal of Democracy and Party Politics, among other journals, and he is a co-author of the book Why Policy Representation Matters (Routledge, 2015).

Tran Van Kham is currently working as an executive editor of Journal of Social Sciences and Humanities, Vietnam National University-Social Sciences and Humanities, Hanoi. He got the PhD in Social Work and Social Policy from University of South Australia in 2012 and had a year as postdoctoral fellow in Seoul National University in 2014. His main research interest and publications related to social inclusion, social constructionism, migrations, public intellectuals, youth studies, disability in Vietnam. He also serves as the international editor of International Social Work Journal and ASEAN Social Work Journal.

Abdul Malik Gismar is the Associate Director of Paramadina Graduate School at Paramadina University – Jakarta, where he also teaches graduate courses in Political Communication. He received his bachelor degree in psychology from University of Indonesia. With Fulbright Scholarship he continued his master degree at the Graduate Faculty of Political and Social Science at the New School for Social Research, New York, USA, where he also received his PhD. His main passion is social and political psychology which includes political decision making and democratic culture. He has served as a member of the Expert Board of the Indonesia Democracy Index (IDI) since 2007. As the Head of the Governance Assessment Unit of the Partnership for Governance Reform (a UNDP project) in 2008 he led the development of Indonesia Governance Index.

Lingling Qi, Ph.D. of Political Science from University of Missouri-Columbia USA (2010), is currently Associate Professor at the School of Government, Nanjing University, China. Qi studies comparative politics, mainly focusing on democracy and democratization, using quantitative methods to analyze civic culture and political institutions. Her articles appear in International Political Science Review, Journal of Chinese Political Science, Asian Journal of Political Science and other Chinese journals.